Reaching In, Reaching Out

Reflections on Reciprocal Mentoring

Dr. Susan Kossak

Copyright © 2011 Susan Kossak

All rights reserved. No part of this book may be used or reproduced by any means, graphic, electronic, or mechanical, including photocopying, recording, taping or by any information storage retrieval system without the written permission of the publisher except in the case of brief quotations embodied in critical articles and reviews.

Balboa Press books may be ordered through booksellers or by contacting:

Balboa Press
A Division of Hay House
1663 Liberty Drive
Bloomington, IN 47403
www.balboapress.com
1-(877) 407-4847

Because of the dynamic nature of the Internet, any Web addresses or links contained in this book may have changed since publication and may no longer be valid. The views expressed in this work are solely those of the author and do not necessarily reflect the views of the publisher, and the publisher hereby disclaims any responsibility for them.

The author of this book does not dispense medical advice or prescribe the use of any technique as a form of treatment for physical, emotional, or medical problems without the advice of a physician, either directly or indirectly. The intent of the author is only to offer information of a general nature to help you in your quest for emotional and spiritual well-being. In the event you use any of the information in this book for yourself, which is your constitutional right, the author and the publisher assume no responsibility for your actions.

Any people depicted in stock imagery provided by Thinkstock are models, and such images are being used for illustrative purposes only.
Certain stock imagery © Thinkstock.

ISBN: 978-1-4525-0163-5 (sc)
ISBN: 978-1-4525-0165-9 (dj)
ISBN: 978-1-4525-0164-2 (e)

Library of Congress Control Number: 2010918087

Printed in the United States of America

Balboa Press rev. date:1/19/2011

Acknowledgements

Think of one thing of value in this world that anyone did alone. Hard isn't it? We are born dependent and strive for independence then wonder is this all there is? If we open ourselves to the universe, incredible people enter our lives at optimal times and we theirs. That's when you know you've grown past *independence* and arrived at the fulfilling state of *interdependence* feeling a sense of belonging to others and them to you.

I am grateful to finally be at that place within myself. And so, I want to acknowledge some very special people who have come into my life at different times when I needed them most and they in turn needed me.

Thank you, Eileen O'Connor, my first editor and writing coach whose organizational skills and love of words guided my writing. Thank you to Chaun Archer for using her creative talents to update my website: www.discoverthepowerofus.com and to design the working cover for this book. These professionals were the very people I needed at the time.

On a personal level I have an unbelievably wonderful group of family and friends rolled into one for whom I am so very thankful. My son, Adam, continues to send positive energy and encouragement all the way from his home in Australia. He is always in my heart. My daughter-in-law, Janie, graciously took on the job of second editor. Her expertise is greatly appreciated. I gained so much more than an editor when she and my younger son, Daniel, married. I got a bright, caring, beautiful daughter. My son, Daniel, supported my spirit through many difficult times and continues to be a constant source of caring and love in my life. Of course, there's my dear, sweet granddaughter, Mattingly, who brings a smile to my face just thinking about her. She's my Sugar Baby and Friday night friend and giggle buddy who brightens my world. Life is full of wonderful surprises for which I am thankful. My life partner, H.D. Saltz and I met at a time in each of our lives when we were ready to see and receive each other's strengths. He increases the love and laughter in my life.

And then, there's Johnnetta McSwain, my mentee, colleague, friend, *sistah,* and constant source of energy and inspiration. Her spirit and determination are contagious.

These relationships are living proof of the power of *interdependence* and the rewards of opening oneself to what the universe provides. L'Chaim! To Life!

Contents

Acknowledgements	v
Introduction	ix
1. Reaching In: The Journey to Johnnetta	1
2. Reaching Out: How the Mentorship Began	9
3. Johnnetta Remembers	21
4. The Qualities of a Mentor: A Look through the Lens of Our Relationship	35
5. A Two-Way Street: The Essentials of a Strong Mentor-Mentee Relationship	43
6. When You Love Yourself It's Easy: How to Keep Going, Accept Setbacks and Embrace Success	47
7. Defining Your Dream and Developing Your Plan	53
8. Relationships: Girlfriends, Family, Men	63
9. Dealing With Conflict	77
10. It's Never Too Late	87
Conclusion: Here We Are, So Now What?	99
Some Frequently Asked Questions on Mentoring	102

Introduction

"What in the hell is a white woman doing here? Why would she even apply to this school? What is *she* going to teach us?"

"I don't know how to explain our relationship. We're friends and colleagues, but you're also still my mentor."

When Johnnetta McSwain, my mentee, spoke those words at different times in our relationship they brought home the realization that relationships are a process and not just a product unto themselves. Relationships are ever-evolving, reciprocal and circular. They are most positive and fruitful when a person is able to be introspective, to reach within herself before reaching outward. Only then can she give to and receive from others. If a relationship is based on mutual respect and honesty, what she receives from the other often inspires further self-reflection, growth, and in turn, giving. A healthy, natural cycle of support is established which helps each person be her best self.

This book is about relationships, particularly the mentoring relationship as seen through the lens of my relationship with my mentee, a woman who herself teaches and inspires me. My relationship with Johnnetta McSwain began with uncertainty. We both were outside our individual comfort zones, each representing unfamiliar territory to the other. It was my initial role as her professor and she as my student in a graduate social work program which placed us in contact on a weekly basis. Johnnetta's innate intelligence, openness, assertiveness and desire to learn made her a teacher's dream student, in spite of her weak academic skills. She hailed from a world wrought with physical and sexual abuse, prostitution, drug dealing and poverty. Johnnetta was in her late thirties, African American, southern,

Christian, and a child of the streets. I was in my sixties, white, northern, Jewish, and a child of a middle class value system. Our backgrounds were distinct, to say the least. Yet, I came to realize that these identifiers are not the true basis for relationships of depth. They simply represent the circumstances and demographics that usually place us in close proximity to others "like" us. People truly connect at a much deeper level when they resonate with one another, when they are at similar emotional places in their life's journey and have similar needs, although these might be expressed in very unique ways.

Whenever I consult, create, or facilitate workshops on mentoring, relationships, or defining and achieving dreams, the number one question asked of me is: "How do I find a mentor?" Other questions related to the qualities of a good mentor and relationship issues quickly follow. I wondered why, with so many programs and books on mentoring available, people still are puzzled. I believe this is because most mentoring work is focused on a formal relationship with a definite hierarchal structure, one in which the mentor imparts wisdom and the mentee absorbs it. The focus is on learning the ropes of the profession or industry, almost as if the mentor is a tutor. If the match is good, it works. However, the desire for a mentor who helps you discover the unique qualities within yourself, who helps you name and realize your dream and supports you through your own ever-changing journey, is usually quite different. For a relationship such as that to happen effectively, the give and take must be reciprocal. This does not imply a rigid 50-50 structure, but rather a natural and circular flow in which each person learns from and teaches the other. This type of human interaction works to the benefit of each and both and is an example of the whole being greater than the sum of its parts.

This book is about such a process. As a professor, consultant, and facilitator I have worked extensively on issues of relationships and diversity. My talent is finding the talent within others. Essentially, *Reaching In, Reaching Out* is about the heart of relationships. While the mentoring relationship is our focus, through our work together Johnnetta and I have learned much about what I consider universal components of all healthy relationships, whether with romantic partners, professional colleagues, family or friends. These key elements are boundaries, respect, care and reciprocity.

The reader will come away with an understanding of essential nuggets of wisdom that will inform their relationship journeys, valuable lessons I have learned with my experience as a mentor, including:

- A healthy relationship with oneself is imperative to forming healthy relationships. The more you value yourself, the more you value others.

- Relationships are not stagnant. They either evolve or dissolve.

- Permeable, ever-adjusting boundaries are essential to all healthy relationships, including one's relationship with self.

- The only relationship we truly go looking for is the relationship with self, and we find our self in others.

I have written this book to share these ideas with you, grounded in the awareness that we understand very little until we get out of our heads and into our guts. That's when we have our "aha!" moments that make all the difference. I have structured this book to that end: after learning where Johnnetta and I both came from and how we found each other in the first two chapters, you will find conversational interviews between Johnnetta and me in which we frankly talk about how our relationship evolved. I believe that wisdom is passed on in conversations, and it is my hope that the book's format allows readers to be present in Johnnetta's living room as we discuss the many facets of relationships and come to new realizations, thus encouraging they experience their own "aha!" moments alongside ours. The concluding chapter shares where we now are at in our individual and collective journeys, and also answers some frequently asked questions I hear in my work as a mentor, professor, trainer, and consultant. I wish you well as you discover the beauty of interdependence on your own path of personal and professional growth.

CHAPTER ONE

Reaching In

The Journey to Johnnetta

"I should have flushed you down the commode! I wish you were never born!"

I shuddered at the cruelty of those cold words and wondered how a mere five-year old had withstood hearing them spoken by her mother. We sat facing each other in my office and she told me about her childhood: a story of abuse and neglect almost unbearable to comprehend.

How did her spirit remain so strong? I listened to Johnnetta, now a vibrant 37-year-old African-American woman and my student in the graduate social work program at Clark Atlanta University (CAU), as she told me of the brutality she had endured and ultimately survived. She had a light that radiated from deep within: from a place, I suspected, of rock-like strength and hard-won wisdom. From her sparkling eyes and authentic smile to the audible joy in her laughter, this light reached out to others and drew them closer, myself included. As I stood in her powerful presence and listened to her speak her truth with dignity and grace, I somehow knew Johnnetta was destined for unusual greatness.

I wanted to assist her in fulfilling that destiny.

Dr. Susan Kossak

How Our Journey Began

It has been four years since I met Johnnetta McSwain and our journey together began. That day was typical of Atlanta's hot, humid Augusts, and student orientation was about to begin. It was hard for me not to stand out in the crowd at CAU. The few non African-American professors did not teach in the School of Social Work, and my strong personality—a penchant for voicing my opinions and "let's get it done yesterday" attitude— only drew further attention. It was time for me to introduce myself to a packed audience of curious faces, and despite the energy with which I usually approach the unknown, my legs began to shake beneath the tightening knot in my stomach. No hiding it, I was anxious.

Whatever could I say to them as an outsider? Mine was the only white face amidst a cohesive group whose bonds were made stronger by intense pride: students and faculty eager to demonstrate the value of their culture, their history, and their school. As I stood before them, my mind frantically searched for a place to begin.

Luckily, my own inner wisdom kicked in with a good dose of common sense: *Don't pretend the 800-pound elephant in the room doesn't exist!* There was no option but to deal with the curiosity and resistance at the onset: To be honest and admit that I wasn't quite sure what I was doing there either. Secretly, I was hoping they could tell me.

"Welcome to Whitney M. Young, Jr., School of Social Work. You're probably wondering what a white professor is doing at a Historically Black College or University (HBCU). Well, with any luck, as you get to know me better, you'll be able to make some sense of it."

There was a light ripple of laughter followed by an audible sigh of relief in the room. It was as if I could hear a collective murmur saying "all right, she's okay."

The Road to Clark Atlanta

As I addressed the students, I couldn't help but reflect on the long road I had traveled to where I stood that day. Radford, the university in the rural Blue Ridge Mountains of Virginia where I had previously taught, was predominately white, but as a Jew from the New York City area, I had been out of my element. Over the years, I consistently cast myself into such "outsider" roles, repeatedly choosing situations that forced me to work to assert my identity rather than submit to being swallowed by the crowd. Teaching in Catholic high schools when my sons were young, for instance, had presented the chance to introduce colleagues and students alike to the joys of bagels and lox, perfect for those Fridays when the nuns were forbidden to eat meat. Maybe the challenging places I have found myself are simply cases of the need for a job usurping my need for comfort, but over the years I have grown more inclined to believe myself a bridge builder, and to think of "spanning gaps" as my vocation.

As to how I arrived at Clark Atlanta University, it seemed most obviously due to my husband's illness. When diagnosed with lung cancer in August 2002, Howard called it a death sentence. "They caught it early," I objected. "And we'll fight this tooth and nail by getting you the best kind of medical care." The best turned out to be a thoracic surgeon in Atlanta. We traveled there from our home in Virginia for the operation, and the doctor pronounced that he "got it all!" No chemo and no radiation were prescribed. We prayed in thanksgiving and dwelled in positive energy however it was offered: at the synagogue with Aunt Fran every Saturday, with Baptist friends who placed Howard's name on their church prayer-chain, and in our own living room as two Buddhist priests performed a healing ceremony.

We counted ourselves among the lucky ones when we toasted the eighteen month mark in his recovery period, the statistical point when the risk of cancer reoccurrence drops off. Soon after that celebration, however, Howard's headaches began, and then came the diagnosis that was our greatest nightmare: Howard had terminal brain cancer. The next month, he underwent two gamma knife surgeries and one incisional brain surgery followed by months of radiation. The arrival of my long-anticipated tenure at Radford University in May 2005 was shadowed by the challenges before us. We sold our home and prepared for our move to Atlanta, where Howard would continue to receive his medical care and where, providentially, my son lived with his young family. When I faced a decision about teaching at another university or returning to clinical social work in Atlanta, fate intervened.

I had been collaborating with the then dean of the School of Social Work at Clark Atlanta University on a study on the use of technology in mentoring students. At the time, I was facing doubts about my curriculum vitae being welcomed at schools where white professors were a rarity, but his urgings convinced me otherwise. And by a stroke of good fortune, CAU's School of Social Work was up for accreditation at the time and needed to diversify their faculty. That made me a well-suited candidate, and I was offered a position.

Within a few short months I was handling the details of a move to another state, a new faculty position and my husband's rapidly deteriorating condition. I arrived at Clark Atlanta feeling stretched to the limits of my endurance as, at sixty-one years of age, I tackled the roles of homemaker, caretaker, and breadwinner in a new environment with minimal income. What held me together was my family's incredible love and support; my granddaughter's love was the balm that soothed my aching soul. And as it turns out, my greatest challenge was to find ways to be kind to myself amidst the struggles that filled my days.

Much of my first year in Atlanta went by in a blur of revolving hospital stays, doctors, ambulances, surgeries, hospice and sleepless nights. During this time, I was also embarking on my first year as a professor at CAU. Although I often felt overburdened by competing responsibilities, I found that teaching kept my spirit from dimming during the darkest times. It was as if helping my students find and nurture their own strengths helped me tap into my own inner light.

During the fall of 2006—the same semester I met a new Master of Social Work (MSW) student named Johnnetta McSwain—my husband's health began to deteriorate rapidly. He passed away on Thursday, December 28. We waited until the Sunday after the Sabbath for a memorial service, which fell on December 31. We closed the service with a prayer at 6 p.m., and at 8 p.m., we opened ourselves to healing and fresh beginnings with a New Year's party at my son's house.

As my sons were now adults, I found myself living alone for the first time in my life. It was finally time for me: I had much life ahead of me to look forward to, but also knew there was much from which to recover. I had been married since the age of twenty-two. I met my husband on a blind date arranged by his sister and my cousin who were classmates at Newark State University, where I also was a student. He proposed after six weeks. My initial answer was "No. I am not ready." I wanted to move to Cambridge, Massachusetts after graduation and find a job there, as I had fallen in love with the city when I took summer courses the previous year at Harvard. But a month later—with no money and an overbearing mother who told me at every opportunity that I would "end up an old maid like Aunt Esther"— I agreed to marry Howard. I dropped out of college with only one year left until graduation. In those days, an education was only necessary for a woman if she couldn't "land" a husband or—"heaven forbid!"— he couldn't support you on his salary. We were married five months after the day we met, and I became pregnant three months later.

I suddenly found myself married, with two sons and numerous responsibilities, and yet no idea of what I wanted. I was unhappy, but divorce was unheard of in my family. I was raised to honor the commitment, and to value the security, of marriage. Perhaps even more strongly was my mother's admonition, "it's up to you to make it work and it's your fault if it doesn't," as well as my father's advice to his daughter for a fulfilling life: "make your husband happy and you'll be happy." And that's what I tried to do.

While our sons Adam and Daniel were still very young I taught at a Catholic High School to save money for a down payment on our first of many houses. As our sons grew we moved to and from a variety of places; over the years we owned over ten houses in New Jersey, California, South Carolina, Virginia and various towns in Florida, usually not staying put for more than three years. Much of this impermanence was due to my husband's instability. On the surface he was very charismatic, but he had no good friends and even admitted he didn't want to have anyone close to him. This extended to our marriage: I knew that he adored me, but we never had deep passion or true emotional intimacy. Although he worked as an analyst for IBM when we were first married, Howard changed positions and careers many times. Around 1985, he started losing jobs due to his increasing emotional volatility. After twenty years of marriage, I learned that Howard was bipolar when he attempted suicide. I suspected that his family had always known. Soon after, I found a note on the toilet seat telling me that he needed time alone and was leaving.

These events coincided with the arrival of my parents to Coral Springs, where we were living at the time. My father was legally blind and my mother had Parkinson's Disease. I was their only source of support. My life consisted of working, going to the nursing home, attending to my parents' laundry, shopping, and personal care needs as well as my responsibilities in my own home, coping with a mentally ill husband, and trying to be a good mother to college kids who weren't getting enough attention.

I felt as if the world were caving in on me, but the ability to feel for long was not an option. I had to stay in my head in order to "hold it together" and forge forward. I was raised to be a middle-class housewife, unprepared to deal with the realities of relationships. I found myself asking "What have I done to bring this on?" After all, I was raised to believe the ills of the world were my doing.

Yet somehow despite this turmoil I had always been ready to seize the opportunity to further my education. Over the years, I was able to finish my Bachelor's degree, earn an MSW and begin my career as a therapist and consultant. And eventually—notably with Howard's encouragement— I earned my doctorate in social work in 1998. For me, learning was a light in the darkness: it was both a nurturing of self and a way to garner wisdom that I could share to better the lives of others. This was one of my first examples of a win-win circle of giving and receiving, what I like to call reciprocal relationships.

During the years before Howard's diagnosis, we went through two more trial separations and attempts at reconciliation. Yet, I supported and cared for him when he became ill. However, as he was dying, many truths were revealed that left me feeling very vulnerable and downright angry. Howard had been lying throughout our entire marriage: he had forged my signature to take $10,000 from my savings and had been day-trading without my knowledge. The dark story of years of reckless financial dishonesty came out when we moved to Atlanta and the day we were going to close on a mortgage, I found out in the lawyer's office that we had significantly less money than Howard had led me to believe. I felt humiliated and foolish. I found myself wondering, "Who have I married?" But even more often I asked myself, "Who have I become? Who was I in the first place?"

Recovering the Self: The Reach In

I like to call the summer of 2007 the best summer of my life. I wasn't teaching and finally had ample time to think about the one person I had been ignoring all my life, myself. I went to counseling, and in a sense began to meet Susan. I reduced the anxiety that had accumulated during so many years of stress, and acknowledged the positives that had come to my life despite so much pain. I read books on spirituality and healing and took long walks; in short, I did whatever I wanted whenever I wanted and enjoyed myself thoroughly. I practiced Feng Shui in my home, opened up passageways for new beginnings, and actually found myself breathing better! I began to tell friends that "it's good to sleep across the bed!" I began to experience a deep connection with myself, and never felt so at peace and comfortable in my own skin.

During this time I got "out of my head" and into my gut: I began to trust my feelings implicitly, and often found myself recalling an amazing experience I had when studying Gestalt therapy at a workshop some twenty years earlier. When I was a small child I always longed for a box of sixty-four crayons. If someone had asked me before the workshop why I had wanted that box of crayons I would have confidently replied, "Because it is the only box that has the silver and gold," knowing that little girls like pretty things that shine. Yet during a Gestalt session the instructor had me sit with my eyes closed and picture something I had wanted during my childhood, and I conjured the image of that box of crayons. "Why did you want that particular box?" he asked. I immediately responded, "Because it had the flesh color." Startled by my own response, I opened my eyes. "Wow!" My body had revealed a truth that my mind had buried: it wasn't the material connection that I sought but rather, the people connection. I didn't crave metallic hues, but rather a shade of human skin. During that same session, the instructor asked me what it would have taken to be valued in my family. My response: "If I had been a boy!"

Looking back on those revelations as I came into my own during the summer of 2007 only drove home the fact that I was not only recovering from events of adulthood, but also from my childhood; the anxiety that "everything is my fault" was deeply rooted in my family's legacy of guilt. I felt no sense of nurturing from my own mother, but she did give me the message that "girls take care of others." I was not my adored older brother, nor was I the first child my parents had lost to spina bifida, who my mother loved to bring up to remind me that if her first daughter had lived then I wouldn't have been born, as she had never wanted more than two children.

I grew up in a second-floor apartment in the Weequahic section of Newark, New Jersey in the 1950s, a neighborhood dotted by little shuls-small storefront Orthodox synagogues- on every corner and kosher delis and butchers alongside them. My parents were first generation Americans, the children of Eastern European immigrants. My father was a chain smoker, heavy drinker, ladies' man and compulsive gambler who at one point almost lost his men's clothing business. My mother was overbearing and critical. Married in November of 1929, one month after Black Thursday, they lost everything at the beginning of the Great Depression. And for sixty years of marriage, they brought out the worst in one another. I was the peacemaker of the family, the one who literally stood between my parents as they fought. My brother was the prince. He was showered with treats like a bicycle, pool table, later a car and any number of "toys" because he was a boy. I was told that girls needed nothing, but did have a bedroom recreated to match my mother's own childhood dream: an organdy spread, a dressing table and rocking chair with a Raggedy Ann doll that could not be touched. When friends came to my house, we couldn't sit on the bed but rather sat on the floor. My mother continually opened the door to check to see that the bed was looking perfect. Yet my brother and his friends would lie on his bed, eat food in his room and do whatever they wanted. I felt unimportant, at times like a hindrance, and that I had to somehow make up for an inherent lack. I believed that I would only be happy if I made others happy first. It was those early lessons that had kept me caretaking my entire life.

Some twenty-five years later, the morning after my initial Gestalt breakthrough, I took a walk and saw a lone flower in the field. I took such joy in spotting its bright petals in the sunlight. I had walked that path the very day before, but I only noticed the flower when I was ready to see it. Healing is like that: life brings us down a path, we may walk a hard road many times over, and then suddenly one day we are ready to really see, to embrace, our entire selves. As my summer of self came to a close, I realized that this hadn't been a vacation but the beginning of a dramatically healthier lifestyle. I knew how crucial my relationship with myself was to having healthy relationships with other people. And at sixty-three years of age, I was finally able to completely own my relationship with myself; to put myself first, before all others. At last I was able to redefine happiness on my own terms and this time I believed my words to the core: "self-love, inner peace, openness, being confident enough to be vulnerable."

After reaching in, I found myself more ready than ever to reach out. I found myself looking forward to fall semester, when the dynamic woman named Johnnetta McSwain would once again be my student.

CHAPTER TWO

Reaching Out

How the Mentorship Began

Flashback to August 2006 when the fall semester—my second at Clark Atlanta— began in the beautifully renovated Thayer Hall Building, the new home of the Whitney M. Young Jr. School of Social Work. My new office had a window overlooking a grassy courtyard, and as I stood in that sun-drenched space watching students on their way to class, I felt a moment of respite from the worries of caring for my sick husband. The openness and luminosity of this new environment, coupled with the excitement of beginning a new semester, filled me with a sense of revitalized possibilities. "It's like opening from darkness into light," I reflected as I looked back to the previous year when I was a stranger to the University and my office was in the windowless basement of Knowles Hall, where the air conditioning, if working at all, was so cold that the secretary sat with a space heater under her desk. Without access to fresh air, or even a view of the parking lot asphalt shimmering beneath Atlanta's 90 degree swelter, I sometimes experienced a suffocating sensation. As if the walls, unyielding and opaque, left no room for me to breathe. This longing for space to simply *be* was exacerbated by the mounting burden of responsibilities and stressors from home I carried upon my shoulders— impossible, as much as I wished, to leave behind me in the school's overcrowded parking lot. I realized how much this positive change in surroundings correlated to my perspectives, and as I prepared to meet my first class I couldn't help but wear a broad smile on my face and walk with spring in my step—something told me that more possibilities and light waited just around the bend.

On one particularly wet day a few weeks later, I rounded that anticipated corner: I shook off the stress of my parking space search and the drench of rain and entered Jazzman Café, where faculty and students alike were congregating in large numbers. The atmosphere immediately recharged my spirits. Animated conversation and echoes of laughter mingled in the air with the scent of banana muffins, and I watched colorful yogurt parfaits topped with crunchy granola being served with abandon. Many students appeared to be tuning out the noise, furiously completing their overdue assignments with their noses to the tables.

Out of the cacophony, I heard a voice call out: "Hey, what's up? Looking good, girl!"

Renee, a student of mine, was greeting the young woman who had stood out from her very first days in my class. Her name was Johnnetta, and today she was holding court in Jazzman amidst a table of captivated classmates. As ever, I was struck by her vibrancy. She was alive with animation. Her manner of speech echoed the streets of her native Birmingham, yet the wisdom of her words engaged her peers—reaching across different worlds, and speaking to varied life experiences. As I observed her from across the bustling café, I saw an unstoppable energy and drive that could call people from all walks of life to attention. Johnnetta was a natural orator and a true leader. Yet she seemed unaware of the incredible light that shone from within her. At that moment I knew I wanted to know her better and began walking towards the table of chattering students.

"Hey there," I called out, "How are you all doing?"

Johnnetta was quick to respond: "Hey, Dr. Kossak, we have some questions about this interview assignment. Can you give us some help? We don't even know where to get a camcorder."

"Can we just audiotape it?" another young woman piped up. "We've never done anything like this before."

"How's it going to be graded?" asked one of the male students, with a look of apprehension.

"Hey guys, don't worry!" Johnnetta spoke up. "Dr. Kossak wouldn't give us something we couldn't do. I'll find a camcorder somehow but," she turned to me with a broad smile, "be easy on us, won't you? I mean, we're no experts."

I liked her candor, the ease with which she spoke her mind. I smiled and reassured them that I would explain the project more fully in class. But I wasn't expecting the barrage of questions that followed:

"What brought you to CAU?"

"We don't get many white professors here."

"What did you study in school?"

"Where are you from?"

Taken aback, I addressed their questions with brevity and a bit of self-consciousness. I suggested that they feel free to stop by my office anytime so that we could get to know each other better. Before walking off, I made sure to recommend the strawberry yogurt parfait. "Just be warned: they're addictive!" Suddenly, I felt growing excitement about the semester ahead. I was connecting with an eager group of students, and I felt a surge of optimism for the first time in many months.

A few weeks later the students in "Autonomous I"— a foundation course for the MSW which grounds students in ethical principles and allows them to practice skills such as writing assessments and interviewing clients— presented the projects they had been eager to ask me about in the Café. The assignment was to videotape a mock interview with a client and critique the strengths and limitations of your skills. Students were graded on their ability to evaluate their performance rather than on their interview skill level. Most had never done much practical work outside of class and were anxious about presenting. Johnnetta's ability to rise to the challenge impressed me. Not only did she take the initiative to borrow a camcorder and do an excellent job on her own project, but she also helped some of her classmates make their recordings. She acted as a self-appointed resource person for the class, a leadership role which would follow her throughout the two-year program. Johnnetta truly shined a bright light into our classroom. She was a role model who brought clarification through her willingness to ask questions, make honest comments, and let her true voice

Dr. Susan Kossak

be heard. She brought inspiration with this openness and her incredible work ethic. Her focus and sincere desire to learn made it both a delight and an honor to be her teacher.

Our student-teacher relationship began to blossom outside of the classroom as well, as Johnnetta started visiting my office. At first, she would come for clarification about an assignment or something that I had said in class. During our conversations, she would sometimes comment about her life or ask me a benign question about mine. As our trust and comfort levels grew, we gradually began to ask each other more, and get to know each other better. It was a natural, gentle progression of interactions, with a sharing of sincere admiration and words of encouragement on both our parts.

As I came to know Johnnetta on a deeper level, I recognized that I was not only giving, but also receiving, from our relationship. I stood on the cusp of change in the fall of 2006: I had weathered many storms, and the waters around me were still choppy. Once, as I walked with Johnnetta to class, I felt overwhelmed by personal stresses and confided that I could use some of her own strength at that moment. I could tell that hearing those words was important to her, as she said that she never realized how others saw her as strong. My husband died on December 28, 2006, when the University was on winter break. When school resumed in January, I shared this news with my classes since they had often inquired about him. Johnnetta rallied her class to purchase and sign a sympathy card, a gesture which was particularly meaningful for me because it revealed the depth of Johnnetta's empathy. Her initiative, so characteristic of her "go-getter" attitude, was the beginning of a deeper bond between us. In spite of our differences in age, race, education, and life background, I sensed a rare symbiosis developing. Our conversations became longer and more frequent, yet, ever respectful of the boundaries that defined our roles. Perhaps our commonality was that we were emotionally in the same place in our life's journey, travelling different paths to the same end. We were both "coming in to our own," so to speak, in terms of personal growth, self-actualization, and acknowledging our own value.

Over time, I learned the details of Johnnetta's story. In class, she was open about sharing details from her own life when they were relevant to the discussion. When we spoke about domestic violence or child abuse, for example, she would offer candidly, "I can understand someone who was sexually molested." Sometimes what she said would bring tears to her eyes, but she was always the first to get her truth out in the open. I sensed that sharing was a part of her healing process, and reinforced that the abuse was not a secret that controlled her. As she started visiting my office more frequently, sometimes three or four times a week, she would mention something from class that directly spoke to her experiences: "I really understood what you said about the impact of sexual abuse…" From there, the conversation would begin, and I might ask her a question to clarify something: "How did you handle that?" or "What happened before?" Because our relationship had boundaries which served as a space for trust to grow over time, Johnnetta felt safe to open the doors that she wanted me to walk through.

Many of those doors led to dark places of memory, revelations of the unthinkable. I learned how Johnnetta and her sister Sonia, older by one year, were raised in Birmingham, Alabama, by an emotionally and physically abusive single mother. At the age of five, Johnnetta, her sister, and a male cousin became the victims of her three uncles, who tied them up and had them perform unspeakable sexual acts. When Johnnetta began wetting the bed because of this trauma, as punishment she was made to sit outside, naked, on the porch of the shack-like house where they lived. Exposed to the elements during long, cold winter nights, she contracted pneumonia as a result. No neighbors, though close enough to hear and see what was occurring, came to her rescue. Throughout her childhood and adolescence, Johnnetta also was abused by the strange men her mother would bring into the different Section 8 houses where they lived for brief spurts of time. Such instability left no room for Johnnetta to learn and develop as most children did, and the living conditions themselves were horrendous. As a young child Johnnetta slept on a small, worn couch in the living room. She recounted details of walls riddled with holes so big that she could see and hear mice running in and out of them, sometimes falling on her as she slept.

In the 11th grade, Johnnetta dropped out of high school and began to work minimum wage jobs at restaurants and warehouses. At age nineteen, she became pregnant with her son and became a welfare recipient.

Despite having no role models from her family or community to show her otherwise, Johnnetta believed that there was a better way to take care of her child and herself than dependence on welfare checks and food stamps, and she tenaciously resolved to make that better way her own reality. She enrolled in a state-funded GED program, attended every class, and passed the exam. She was a speaker at the commencement ceremony, a very proud moment for her despite the absence of her family. Johnnetta then enrolled in community college and worked part-time jobs until becoming pregnant at age twenty-five with her second son and again dropping out of school. But a month after giving birth, she began taking classes at the state-funded Computer Institute, which gave her skills such as resume writing, job interviewing, and word processing, allowing her to work for temp agencies as an administrative assistant and make above minimum wages for the first time.

Yet despite the improvements she had made to her young family's situation, Johnnetta was not satisfied. She knew that she and her sons deserved more, and most importantly, she believed that she herself could achieve more. At age thirty-two, realizing she still was a product of an environment marked by every social ill and inequality imaginable, she made a crucial decision to move to Atlanta with the goal of becoming the first in her family to earn a four-year college degree. On March 5, 2002, she rented a truck, packed all her belongings, and drove to Atlanta twice in the same night. Once in Atlanta, Johnnetta applied to Kennesaw State University. In January 2003, she began classes fulltime, including summers, and graduated May 11, 2006. In just three years, she had earned a B.S. in Communications. In the fall of 2006, she began Clark Atlanta University's Social Work program to pursue her MSW.

I knew this powerful story needed to be told. During her second semester as my student, I began to encourage Johnnetta to share her journey with others in more formal settings. Her own experience was ripe with practical wisdom that people could utilize to improve their own lives as well as those of others. Johnnetta set to work and created an empowerment workshop for women, which she, myself and another CAU faculty member presented to the Georgia Chapter of the National Association of Social Workers in October 2007. The 12-step workshop, titled "Breaking the Cycle, Beating the Odds," teaches women self-awareness and empowerment so that they can recognize and end negative patterns in their lives. Johnnetta conceived of the workshop format—a "Self-Awareness Model" that offers guidelines to help women from all walks of life recognize and break away from the seemingly incessant effects of traumatic life experiences— when someone asked her if she had ever gone through a 12-step addiction program. She answered no, that despite the other self-destructive behaviors she had engaged in on the streets, she had never done hard drugs or abused alcohol. "Why did someone think, other than the environment I came from, that I was addicted to something?" she recalled to me. "Then I realized that, yes, I was addicted— to negative cycles of behavior. I was addicted to the streets." Johnnetta admitted that despite how far she had come, when she returns to Birmingham for visits, she feels a pull toward that life again, despite all her accomplishments. "Some people are addicted to abusive relationships or self-destructive behaviors," she said. "These kinds of cycles of negative behavior are addictions that need to be broken." She thus turned her own experiences into the Self Awareness Model for overcoming abusive cycles, negative scripts and self-hatred. The workshop nurtures awareness of inner strengths that can be used to overcome these odds and attain self-worth and wellbeing.

Like "Breaking the Cycle, Beating the Odds," many of the projects Johnnetta and I pursued as mentor and mentee grew from seeds planted during our conversations. Our relationship helped nurture empowering realizations, "aha!" moments that we felt should be shared with others. For example, we recognized the importance of having a "bottom line" when I asked Johnnetta what she thought was the difference between herself and her sister, who was still on the streets, using crack, and HIV-positive. Johnnetta responded that although she had hung out with drug dealers and gang members and even prostituted herself on the streets, she never allowed herself to do drugs. "That was your safety net, your bottom line," I told her, "You had a floor, your sister didn't." And just like that, we began to brainstorm ideas for a workshop about setting a bottom line for teenage girls. A particularly important moment occurred in my sun-filled office one afternoon in the spring of 2008. We were talking about how to take the 12 steps of "Breaking the Cycle" to the next level in another workshop for women's empowerment. In workshops and in class, we were always asked about the next steps, about how to move forward and attain change after gaining awareness. That day we talked about the importance of having a goal to move towards, and how one defines a dream. I asked Johnnetta why she had left Birmingham and she responded she wanted an education, and that she had been compelled by a desire to feel valued, as opposed to ignored or looked down upon. We spoke about education being the means to that feeling of self-worth, and thus, we began to design a workshop titled "What's the Plan?," which guides participants in visualizing their dreams and developing concrete plans to attain them.

Dr. Susan Kossak

Johnnetta's workshops were truly powerful and healing for all who attended. Enthusiastic response about how "for real" and inspirational she was always followed a presentation. In the words of one participant, "I was on the verge of tears, I laughed, and I kept thinking how every woman needs to hear Johnnetta speak." The more I witnessed Johnnetta's ability to reach, move and motivate others through her story, I knew just how true these sentiments were, and heard in them a mandate to help Johnnetta's powerful story reach more people. In April 2008, I took the initiative to call Georgia Public Broadcasting and tell them about Johnnetta's empowering story, adding that "Johnnetta is the type of person you really have to meet in person in addition to reading her information." As fate would have it, GPB was in the planning stages for a documentary on child abuse and neglect, and the executive producer Pam Roberts agreed to come to my office to meet Johnnetta. What was scheduled as a half hour meeting turned into a discussion of over two hours, and Pam Roberts found Johnnetta's story of transcending years of brutal treatment so compelling that she chose to focus the documentary on Johnnetta and another survivor of child abuse living in Georgia named Michael McClain. Narrated by Jane Fonda, *The Road Beyond Abuse* uses their two stories to examine how and why these two adults, despite enduring severe physical and emotional traumas, were able to recover and create healthy lives for themselves.

I accompanied Johnnetta for the taping in Birmingham, Alabama, and we visited the house—an empty boarded-up shack with a cement floor—where the abuse occurred. Being in that place together is one of the most powerful moments we have shared. The male cousin who had been tied up with Johnnetta and her sister was living there, and Johnnetta was interviewed on the same porch steps where she was forced to sit naked through the night. We walked around the neighborhood. Johnnetta pointed out different drug dealers and explained to me what was happening on the streets. We met some teachers at the high school from which Johnnetta had dropped out. We visited her sister's project apartment; Sonia was so proud, especially of the curtains she had bought for the windows, after being homeless for so long. We also went to Johnnetta's mother's house, which was so packed with clutter we could hardly walk in the door.

The Road Beyond Abuse was broadcast on April 15, 2009. The following Friday, Kennesaw State University, where Johnnetta had earned her undergraduate degree, threw a reception in her honor, complete with a panel discussion and a screening of the documentary. That same month,

Johnnetta was awarded "Phenomenal Woman of the Year" by Kennesaw State University. At the reception, she was presented with a beautiful plaque and learned that the school was starting a scholarship for women in her honor.

Since then, Johnnetta and I have spoken about mentoring on Clark Atlanta University television and radio, as well as Georgia Public Broadcasting radio. We have created dvd workshops together, and I have advised her in founding "Breaking the Cycle Beating the Odds," a nonprofit organization dedicated to empowering women to break negative cycles and reach their fullest potentials. Johnnetta has been traveling to local and national conferences to present her 12-step Self Awareness Model, including at the National Association of Social Workers Conference, and also speaks to audiences at churches, schools and colleges. As mentor and mentee, we have had the opportunity to make connections with women from a variety of fields and walks of life who are doing positive work in this world. Last November, Johnnetta and I traveled to New York City to brainstorm about a UN-sponsored "Women's World" conference, opportunities to work with the UN Commission on the Status of Women and the Stop Violence Against Women Movement, and a conference in New York about empowering women. That night, we sat down for dinner in Manhattan with a group of dynamic women, including a photographer, a psychologist, a homeopath and humanitarian—all such accomplished, warm, and welcoming women. Johnnetta later told me that feeling herself a valued member of that circle was empowering. For me, as her mentor, it was a joyously tearful occasion, the culmination of a wonderful visit which reinforced my belief in the possibility of people reinventing themselves and transforming themselves against all odds.

Johnnetta graduated from Clark Atlanta University School of Social Work, with a GPA of 3.95, in May 2008. The honors she earned did not surprise me, as I had witnessed for two years the passion with which Johnnetta pursued her education. She went above and beyond, attending any available continuing education workshops despite her demanding schedule as mother of two and utilizing the writing center regularly to make great strides in improving her writing skills. In Fall 2010, she entered the doctoral program in Social Work at Clark Atlanta, coinciding with the release of her first book, an autobiography titled *Rising Above the Scars*.

Dr. Susan Kossak

Mentoring Essentials: Initial Thoughts on a Unique Relationship

As we grew in our personal and professional relationship, Johnnetta and I evolved from student and teacher to mentor and mentee. We are now also friends and colleagues, with our old and new roles often times overlapping. Johnnetta often says, "I don't know how to explain our relationship. We're friends and colleagues, but you're also still my mentor." I agree, and remind her that our roles are reciprocal. Time after time I learn something new from her. She has introduced me to the rich music, foods and customs of her culture, taught me about unrelenting energy and survival skills, shown me the power of creativity when coupled with street-smarts, and demonstrated how networking abilities can be used to nurture supportive communities out of seemingly disparate individuals. Some people are surprised, given the closeness of our bond, that Johnnetta still can't bring herself to call me by my first name. Even though I have asked her many times, she insists on calling me Dr. Kossak. The culture in the classroom at Clark Atlanta University is formal, and titles of respect are important. Professors are addressed as "Doctor", and students as "Mister" or, in Johnnetta's case, Ms. McSwain. It is something we laugh about together—the fact that Johnnetta will invite me to a "girls' night" jewelry party at her house but won't call me Susan, even in private. But it is also a good example of the boundaries that were in place at the beginning of our relationship, and which have evolved and expanded and ultimately, we believe, helped us to grow closer.

In a sense, boundaries have served as a safety net for our relationship as mentor and mentee. As humans we share of ourselves when we feel secure, and boundaries—whether articulated or understood—define a safe space. Trust comes and goes too quickly without boundaries to provide structure, nurture confidence in one another, and let us know the parameters of the relationship so that we let it develop naturally, over time, without losing ourselves in the process. Boundaries are not rigid, they evolve. As trust grows the boundaries expand.

I have been asked many times about the difference between being someone's therapist and being a mentor. For one, Johnnetta and I respect each others' personal lives; she feels comfortable coming to me about any situation that she wants to discuss, but that is rarely for flat-out advice about a personal problem. As someone who literally raised herself and found her own means to survive, Johnnetta is very self-sufficient. She might share what she is going through, but she never is at-sea about what to do. Rather, we tend to sit together and think through ways that she can approach a broader issue. Many times a mentor-mentee conversation is akin to how one would share with a friend; sometimes a friend is just there to listen, and that is all you need, and sometimes you are seeking a suggestion, a new idea, for the questions that have been cycling through your mind to be cast in a fresh light.

I believe our relationship works so well because it is motivated by interdependence rather than independence or dependence. For someone to be in a healthy relationship, they have to possess a strong sense of self, know their own strengths and limitations, recognize that every person needs support in some way, and feel comfortable asking for that support. Interdependence, the essence of a mentoring relationship, is a give and take. That vital element of reciprocity is in place. It's as simple as saying: "I need other people and I know that other people need me."

A Guide for Those Who Would Guide: The Story of this Book

Johnnetta and I are two people who give to each other, who see each other's unique gifts. I was encouraged by colleagues, students and particularly by Johnnetta to use our own story as a way to teach people about the mentoring relationship, particularly the importance of both people being open to learning from each other, valuing other ways of knowing, willingness to be vulnerable, and risking growth. Because mentoring is not a simple academic exercise, but rather a give and take that comes from the heart, I decided that an interview format would be the best means of sharing our journey and perspectives with the reader. A dialogue seemed to be the most honest way to maintain our voices, and allow the readers to take away the information that resonates with them. This story of mentoring and reciprocal learning isn't about everything we have accomplished together, but rather about how we achieved what we did through the mentoring relationship. As such, the chapters that follow are comprised of conversations we had during many afternoons spent at Johnnetta's home in the summer of 2009. Over lunch and often outbursts of laughter, we discussed many topics, including how to define the roles of mentor and mentee, the importance of reciprocity in relationships, dealing with conflicts, and nurturing, above all, a relationship with oneself. As such, this book not only serves as a resource for those who want to learn the ins and outs of mentoring, but also it was my intention to offer a broader

Dr. Susan Kossak

reflection on the interdependence of all of us, and how to make this world a better place one relationship at a time.

CHAPTER THREE

Johnnetta Remembers

In this conversation, Johnnetta reflects upon the natural progression of our relationship from student and teacher to mentee and mentor. She shares her initial reactions to having a white woman, myself, as her professor at an historically black university. We also listen to Johnnetta talk about her life before she was a student at Clark Atlanta University: she recalls her brutal childhood and young adulthood on the streets of Birmingham, Alabama, and the life-changing decision to move to Atlanta when she was 32 years old. Other topics we touch upon include the place of spirituality in knowing and fulfilling one's life purpose, and the strengths and resources one develops during difficult times that later can be channeled towards creating a better future.

Susan: We've come so far since that first day. Our relationship has strengthened as our emotional connection has grown. I know that many of our boundaries are evolving as our relationship deepens. If you would, please share your recollections of our first encounter at Clark Atlanta University.

Johnnetta: I was nervous and excited. Based on what I knew about HBCUs, I never thought I would see anyone like you there. I thought "What in the hell is a white woman doing here? Why would she even apply to this school? What is *she* going to teach us?" I thought about what boring speeches were coming our way, but when you got up to speak, you broke the ice right away.

Dr. Susan Kossak

You said something like, "You're probably wondering what I'm doing here, especially knowing the rich history of the Whitney M. Young, Jr. School of Social Work, Clark Atlanta University, and the Afrocentric perspective. Well, I hope as you get to know me better, you'll be able to answer that question for yourself. Perhaps you'll then share it with me." And I felt less anxious. It's true, you were just another professor, but to me, there was something special about you being willing to teach in a black school. You showed me that you were taking on a challenge – and I love challenges more than almost anything.

I knew you were dealing with students from poor backgrounds, and that this situation was not conducive to the process of education. Many of these students were younger, just out of their parents' homes and some were, well, nontraditional students. They were from different backgrounds than you. Some students had minimal life experience. I know, too, that HBCUs don't pay as much as other schools, so to me it was clear you were special from the start. I didn't know anything else about you. You looked rich, not in terms of money, but like a professional. Where I come from, that is looked on as greatness.

Normally, you expect a black person to be teaching at a black school. But what is "abnormal" can be good—it brings a different perspective. And, in this case, it definitely was a good thing, because you saw every student as having an opportunity to be their best.

I came in knowing I didn't expect a hand-out. I came from a place of being on welfare and food stamps and I had a vision of leaving all that behind. I wanted to really earn everything I got, and I really wanted to do well. I graduated from Kennesaw State University with a 2.5 GPA, mostly because I didn't do well in sciences, but I told myself I would graduate from CAU with honors.

Susan: How did you do at CAU? How was your experience there?

Johnnetta: I was looking forward to learning. I had life skills but no social work background. I chose to study social work because I wanted to help people. I felt I had a message and knew that social workers worked in my community, so I thought it would be a way for me to give back. Despite the fact that I didn't have a strong educational background coming into CAU, it was great. I met new people. I developed new skills I could use. In your classes, I learned how to conduct interviews, assess clients, and worked a lot on my presentation skills. I use these skills now for social work, but I use them in a lot of other places. They have definitely helped me to create and give my workshops! And the fact that it is an HBCU meant it offered a good sense of community. I loved coming to the campus. Parking next to the projects, going to school right next to the poor part of town, reminded me where I was from. I could walk over to the "dope man" on the corner or start talking to someone in the classroom and not feel threatened by either. I realized I could use my street-smarts in other ways. For one thing, it helps with networking, because I know how to read people.

I remember in your "Autonomous Practice" class, I was thinking: "What on Earth is this woman talking about?" The truth is that I was scared. The first assignment, the interview, was frustrating. We didn't have a clue, and the folks at the library couldn't help us, either. What saved us was that my friend had a camcorder. I remember that you wrote all the while that we presented. That made us nervous. *What could she be writing?*

The way you handled the classes showed us that you trusted our maturity, and it allowed for open discussion of some hotly debated topics. It made me really enjoy coming to school each day. And the Afrocentric perspective you integrated into the assignments made them important to us and showed respect for our culture.

You certainly were not what I expected a white professor to be. You knew so much about our history. You could relate to everything, and you always had your theories. I just never met anyone like you before. I had white professors but they were not like you. You could always speak about things in ways we could relate to. I like your approach, "hands on." Some students didn't though, mostly because they were lazy. There were also students who came to class for reasons other than wanting to be there. Some of them were struggling, uninterested, had other priorities. But I knew I needed to learn something. I was only doing this one time.

I sat in Jazzman Café all the time and I'd see you racing by. You were always in a hurry. *Where is she rushing to...?* One day you stopped to get your breakfast, and you told me: "You should do something with women."

And, that was it for me. That day changed my life. That was a time in my life when I was trying to find Johnnetta McSwain. I had a communications degree, but I knew that something was still missing.

Dr. Susan Kossak

I didn't know what to do or where to go next. I needed someone in my life who just accepted me, someone I didn't need to build up, someone to talk and laugh with and help me find me and uncover my fears. I needed somebody special, not like my friends who judge me.

I have a strong personality, I can admit that. I have always been a hard worker, too. I needed someone who understood those things. When you came into the lunch room and mentioned how much I bring to the class, I felt welcomed. *She took the time to think about what I bring and who I am. She knows something about me.* I was thrilled when you suggested working with me: "We should get together and do something for women."

That was all I needed to hear.

I wouldn't have come up to you. It was your actions that made me realize I mattered to you. So, I felt I could come and knock on your door, like we were friends; yet, I always respected you on an even higher level.

One day, you made a proposal: "Hey, what about writing your own story? I'll be happy to help you with it."

Well, at that point, I didn't want to write alone; but more than that, I didn't want to write with you. I guess I was mostly afraid of disappointing you. And when you sensed my fear, you said, "Just go from your gut. It's your story." Those words really helped.

I often think today that if you didn't give me that paper to write, everything would be different. I would never have thought of the 12-steps, my Self-Awareness Model. I definitely wouldn't have written them down.

It was especially significant when you gave me your home phone number in case I needed help. Little by little, you opened up to me ... and me to you.

You seemed to "get me" like no one else ever had. I would laugh to myself, *maybe she read the personal statement I had written for my application*! I knew you thought I could do it, and that's what kept me coming to that cold office of yours all the time. It was there that I talked about my personal dreams with you.

Susan: Speaking of personal statement, can you tell us a little bit about your background and life and especially your move to Atlanta?

Johnnetta: I'm from a very poor part of Birmingham, Alabama. It was an abusive childhood. The abuse was the whole nine yards: sexual abuse, physical abuse, emotional abuse. I spent most of my time between my grandmother's house and with my mother, when I saw my mother. I can remember from the age of about three or four spending most of the time at my grandmother's house. Momma just dropped us off and kept going. The sexual abuse started at about five. It happened to me, my sister and my little boy cousin. Three of our uncles tied us to chairs and made us perform all kinds of sexual acts. They raped us, and made us watch the others being abused too. At that time my mother was in and out. She came every nine or ten days. My mother was an alcoholic, drunk all the time and acting like a fool, just crazy. My grandmother was sick all the time. She was on dialysis. My grandfather had diabetes. There was no love or anything like that.

We moved a lot, about every two years. We moved from school to school. Momma was the kind of Momma who dragged you everywhere. If she went to jail, you went with her, if she went to the bootleg house you got dragged there with her. If we weren't with Momma or at Grandmomma's house, we were alone. In those days, they left the kids home alone. We locked the door and didn't open for anybody. No one knew you were there. You can't do that today. There is a law against it now and there was then too but nobody paid attention to it. Pretty much we lived on Section 8 housing. We were on food stamps, welfare, all of it. The most my Momma worked, and she did work, was three days a week. She worked "over the mountain." "Over the mountain" where I come from is where the rich people lived. She worked two or three days a week and then she went to school and got her certificate in cooking. She's an excellent cook. So, that's one good thing she gave us—we had to learn how to cook. She started working at the Marriot when we were in about sixth grade cooking and she worked there for a very long time. So, she always did something, so that is something I can give her.

We never were settled in one school. My sister started acting out, I'd say from about the seventh grade. We didn't know what was wrong with her. She began fighting. She stole my grandmother's gun. She ran away from home. She tried to fight my Momma. It was horrible. And I think it was a cry for some kind of help. Of course, I'm in the background, seeing all of this and I knew I couldn't act like my sister was because my mother wasn't going to change. It wasn't worth it to me. I didn't need her approval.

I thought she was a fool! It was at that time too that we started going to church. We went to church five nights a week. We were heavily involved in it.

Susan: But, the church didn't intervene with all the abuse happening?

Johnnetta: They didn't know. Or more likely they didn't ask any questions, because they didn't want to know. My mother was in and out of the church. My mother might go to church for three or four years and then she would stop and come back years later. People from the church would pick me and my sister up at our house and take us there. But, I will say that the abuse wasn't as bad when my Momma was going to church. You didn't get called bitches and hos. She didn't smoke, fight or drink. She didn't bring home all sorts of boyfriends who abused you too. So, it was much better. We were grateful she was going to church then. Now, she's back in the church. She's a much calmer person. She's the way you saw her. That's the best she's been. I learned a lot from the church even though I went down my own road of self-destruction. There were a lot of things I didn't do because of church. I had my bottom line. It's just amazing that I didn't put a pipe in my mouth, or that when I was hooking I always listened to my gut and didn't get into certain cars. I had a good sense of people, a good instinct, and no matter what I was doing I always followed it. When I was doing the lowest things I remembered being told in the church that "this is degrading, this is not godly." It never left me and I am grateful to this day that I went to church.

Susan: It helped you develop a conscience?

Johnnetta: Yes, but not just conscience. It gave me a sense of God, of spirituality. Everyone needs some spirituality in their lives, period. Spirituality gives me balance in the things I do today in my life. But, at that time I probably didn't want it. I wanted to be a normal girl in my teens. I wanted to go to movies and wear my little chic jeans, ya know? I wanted to go out and be one of the girls because I was always picked on. You know, "You're ugly, you're this and that." I just wanted to be like them. I wanted to be cute. I wanted to wear lip gloss. I couldn't because my mother wanted to present a good image to the people in church. So, I had to sneak it, which I think, made it more fun. We had to sneak to go to the skating rink, sneak to go to see a boy. But, that was a big thing for my sister and me. We were treated so bad in the church too because, well, my mother would never take up for us. She would let people criticize her children and never say a word.

Susan: How did you get treated badly in the church?

Johnnetta: We were pointed at as the kids in the church who weren't as good as other kids. Not that we were bad, but we weren't as good as other kids. I'm going to say it that way.

Susan: In what way weren't you as good?

Johnnetta: My sister got pregnant at fourteen. She was fighting all the time, acting like a fool. The parent is supposed to be the parent in the home, so when my sister got pregnant my mother was embarrassed. Who wants their kid pregnant at fourteen? They would bad mouth us, and my mother never took up for us. She acted like she didn't give a damn about us. You have two kids and you need to stand up for them. But, she never did. I think that's always been an issue for us, especially for my sister. It hurt too much, we were just teenagers.

So I lost hope. I needed clothes, underwear, a job. I was getting bad grades in school. My momma gave up on us. I was out there in the streets and when you're getting love from the streets, you're not going to get nurturing with it. You're going to get the hard core streets and that's it. The pipe dreams that the men are going to sell you, the babies, everything. Because it's not coming from a nurturing person, it's coming from the streets. But at the time you say "hey, this looks good. This is going to make me feel good." When in reality it's not. So, yeah, at sixteen, seventeen years old I lived right next to the dope house. I woke up everyday and was able to see what was happening. That was in the 80's when crack cocaine was the biggest and the rocks came out and everyone was buying it. You were amazed that the dope man was making a thousand dollars a day! Hey, that was a lot of money! That was magical for me. And, of course, those were my homeboys. We kicked it, as we'd like to say. So, my homeboys would say, "Want to make some money?" Of course I wanted to make some money! I started becoming a little dope girl, selling dope. You know, I had a gun. I think about it now and you couldn't even pay me. But I was the scariest person on the block. Anyone who knew me would tell you that. I was acting like a fool. I was hanging out with some of my homeboys who were notorious for carrying AKAs and they were killing people right in front of me. Being on the streets like that is scary but exciting in the sense of giving you a rush. Talk about changing from toting a bible to toting a gun!

Susan: Did you ever shoot anyone?

Johnnetta: No, not me. But, they were fools. They did. I'm not making this up. That's the way it was. Everything about the hood is survival. It's just one word, *survival*. It's me or you. It's not that you're a bad person, it's just the streets are all you know. Your momma sold dope or your momma smoked dope. It's either you smoked dope, bought dope or sold dope. I'm just being honest. Their mommas can't pay their bills and then they're out there selling dope and buying their mommas cars and houses. That's what they do. That's just the way it is. The basketball stars, the rappers, they get rich and buy their mommas things cause they saw them suffer. My momma couldn't buy me shoes, simple shoes from Payless. We didn't have parents who taught us about education, who read a newspaper, or anything. All we did was hear our mommas cuss and fuss, fight, play cards or put the blues on and that's it. There was nothing about going to school and being something. Again, that's the streets and it will kill you. It's all about survival and making it to another day. If you get a bullet wound, then you are the "shit." You are a warrior. I know it's crazy but it's absolutely the truth.

I love who I am. I love where I come from. I wouldn't change it. I wouldn't trade it. I know people say "What? You wouldn't trade it?" No, it made me the woman I am today: this person who spills out with glee in my workshops. I'm so happy because I know who I am and where I come from. I can sit with the best of the best and I can get down with the best too. I love that about me. I feel so sorry for people who haven't got a clue how to survive. "Oh my God, I lost my job! I'm going to kill myself." *What? Girl, you have a rent party and we're going to get it up!* Someone hosts a party, and everyone brings something to eat or drink and a little something for your rent. Our mentality is simple.

I love being able to look, listen and just chill out. I love when people try to play me because I've been a player for a long time so I know the game. I love when people try to get around me. People don't know how to take me. Because when you think you got me figured out I'm going to give you something else to think about. I love having the education I do because for me the goal was not to do research or surveys or write textbooks but to go back into my community with something other than a baby, a gunshot wound, three tattoos, three baby daddies, and the biggest house on the corner. To go back with the credentials they thought I couldn't get because I was too ghetto, because I couldn't talk right or didn't know how to act. I love proving, no not proving but being a messenger, a true messenger for the people in the community. I can't go into the community and talk about nineteen theories. Who gives a damn? I still need to go into the community and stand in the dope man's face and speak his language, to go to the beauty shop and speak the language there, to go to the heart of the ghetto.

Susan: What's the "language" in the beauty shop?

Johnnetta: You know, being able to sit and talk like regular people. No one wants you to come in and you are this "doctor somebody." A credential don't matter in the hood. It don't matter. It's just going to intimidate the next person. You need to know how to use the credentials to empower. Use it for good. I go home and everybody gathered around me when I said I was getting married. They all asked, "Oh, Johnnetta do you love him?" because before I didn't love anybody. All of the women's faces lit up because I could love someone. It empowered them. They're proud when they see someone like themselves change. They're not going to change. "I'm going to keep on smoking my blunts, girl. I'm going to keep on popping these pills. I'm going to keep on layin' up and keep on having these babies. I'm going to stay in the hood. I'm going to stay doing what I'm doing, but when we look at you we know this can happen." So, I go not to change anyone but to show what can be done. They don't even ask me to smoke a blunt. It's respect. It's never "who do you think you are, bitch?" It's "look at Johnnetta!" and it's just happiness from them. That lets you know that you crossed over, that you've made it out of there and you're respected. So, I can go right now and say, "What's up baby girl? What's shaking, ya know?" and you speak their language and they'll hang with you. You're safe with them and the average person wouldn't be. Then I can walk into the board room and talk about the Afrocentric Perspective and be just as comfortable. My background plays a significant part.

Susan: So, you see the strengths you received from your background as well as the limitations.

Johnnetta: And, there are limitations, but I know me and I know who I am.

Susan: How is it that you recognize your skills and know who you are and a lot of people who come from your background don't?

Johnnetta: Well, I'm not the only one who comes from the hood and has a miraculous story. There are people who were Crips and Bloods and are now doctors and lawyers. We know when we come from the hood that we need to go back. It's a message that's clear. You see the football or basketball player who had a single mom who suffered, so once he makes it he goes back and gives to other women. If we don't give back the community will talk about us real bad. We know we got to do it, there's no compromise. The question is how. I'm doing the Johnnetta McSwain scholarship. I have to do that. I'm nothing if I can't give to my community. I want to take a bus load of kids somewhere. I want to get them book bags. I can't wait to go into a restaurant and leave a thousand dollar tip the way Tyler Perry does. I can't wait to watch something on TV about a person suffering and give ten or fifteen thousand dollars to them. They don't have to be African American, it's about the cause. Giving back is what it's about. It's reciprocal, as you'd say. You are so blessed when you give.

Susan: Tell me about where you are today.

Johnnetta: Oh, today I'm a whole lot of places. Right now I can't even put it in words how I feel. I am living my dream! I'm living my purpose and how many people can wake up every day and no matter how they feel, how dark the day looks, how weary they get, can say that?

Susan: And how would you define your purpose?

Johnnetta: My purpose, especially now, is to travel and give all of this joy to others. When I get the mic in my hand and jump up and look into the eyes of my attendees and see sixty, sixty-five people there to hear Johnnetta McSwain, the feeling is so overwhelming and so real that it's almost like an out of body experience.

Susan: So, is it egotistical?

Johnnetta: No, it's appreciative. It's gratefulness. Here's another sixty people that I'm going to be able to touch. That's what it is. It's living your purpose, your dream. I've never thought about the ego part. The confidence, yes. The confidence is there. I rarely get nervous because I know my message. It's there and it's gonna flow because when you are ordained to do something you don't ask "why me?" You say "why not me?" and you do it.

Susan: Who ordained you to do this?

Johnnetta: I believe in my heart that I was born to live the life I live, to be 39 years old and have the message that I've got. Everyone has a story, but nobody tells their story like I tell mine. Nobody! And I know it's a gift. People walk up to me and say, "No one reaches an audience like you." I got an e-mail from Missouri asking me to send them a short description of my speech. I said, "I don't have one. I don't know what I'm going to say until you introduce me and give me the mic. So, I'm only going to think about the Hope Conference when I'm on the airplane flying out.

Susan: Okay, I'm going back and I'm going to play the devil's advocate. What did you always say when your associate Keisha constantly used "God told me" as an explanation for everything?

Johnnetta: Well, it was a bit over the top for me, you know? Some people use "God" as an excuse, when they haven't done any work themselves. Keisha's not me and I can only talk about my own relationship to God because I'm living it. And, I couldn't do this without God. But my God helps those who help themselves. In my workshops I don't usually use the word "God" but sometimes I have to because he doesn't deny me and I don't deny him. I usually say your higher power, your spiritual being, but we are sitting in my house right now so I can say God. I don't care what other people say about God, but I wouldn't be sitting here without Him. At 30 years old I didn't have someone to tell me that something was wrong. I stood in the mirror and said "something's wrong." I couldn't have done this without God. He spared my life when I was running the streets and dropping in and out of john's cars in all these really bad neighborhoods, where I could have been shot or stabbed.

Susan: So, where was God to protect you from your uncles?

Johnnetta: He protected me.

Susan: How?

Dr. Susan Kossak

Johnnetta: God is always with us. I don't think He ever leaves us. What happened to me happened. I think there was a reason. That was meant to be my history. I think there is good that has come out of it. It was the same way with Job. He never cursed God. He was there with me. He protected me. Worse things could've happened. I'm not going to be mad and angry. I'm not going to do that. For what? I have to be where I'm at— recognize what was done to me and not be in denial. But I am not going to waste my energy on it, because I also have sense. He gave us sense, five of them.

I am not always bringing God into everything, though. Business is business, and I don't go to church the way I used to. I don't claim to be this disciple who "heard from Him" and that kind of thing. But, I do know why I'm here. I've got enough sense to know that I've got to eat and pay bills and I got enough sense to stand up for myself. I don't twiddle my thumbs and wait for God to tell me what to do. I get up off my ass and do what I need to do. I'm not the type of person who is going to pray to the clouds with a prayer cloth on all day and wish and hope. No! I'm not like my Mom who goes to church and just like that she's saved and can say "see, I'm a good person!" I'm like you. I'm not one to judge anybody's beliefs. And I don't think you should beat people over the head with your own beliefs. One thing I do in my workshops and speaking engagements is say *my* God or a spiritual being. I think that's appropriate to say.

Susan: Do you ever face criticism for what you say at your workshops?

Johnnetta: Well, when people say things like "the white man got me down," I feel that it's my job to clear that up. "The white man got me down"? Oh, no! I'm not going to allow you to say it around me. I'm not going to allow you to say education is nothing but a piece of paper. You bring that shit to the street, but you don't bring that attitude in here. And I get criticism from some African Americans that I am helping whites through my documentary, that I am making them look good when the truth is that more white than black people helped me. And some say I am not a good representation of the community because of my grammar or my way of being really outspoken. They might doubt that I am really a doctoral student. From whites the criticism is not blatant, but in the past I have felt looked down upon for being poor and for what I was doing on the streets, and now and then I will still hear a racist comment. So, I have gotten criticism from both races, but that's okay. When you get educated, when you learn something, you need to pass it on. You need to speak your mind. You don't just say "I agree with you" when you actually don't. No, you say, "I don't agree with that!"

At a workshop someone once said they thought an abuser can still be a great father even though he's a lousy boyfriend. No, I don't agree with that. This has nothing to do with what it says in some book, this just has to do with damn common sense. What's your definition of great? Because when a father puts his foot in a child's momma's ass that child don't think their daddy's great. Let me tell you. I've been a child and peeked around the corner and seen my Momma getting knocked around and my sister crying. Do you think we thought that man was great? He took us to McDonalds and bought us ice cream and a cheeseburger, but did we think he was great? Hell to the no!

So, to wrap it all up, you can stand up for your beliefs and be open-minded at the same time. I'm very open-minded. I rarely get upset, and I accept people's opinions. You answer to your name. When someone calls and it's not your name, you don't answer because it's not you. What I mean by that is if someone calls you a jerk, why even respond? You know better than anybody who you are and what your value is. You don't have to believe people's negativity, let it get under your skin and stop you from being who you are. I had to learn that if people aren't going to like you, then they're not. I accept it. I had a woman in one of my workshops twisting and turning, looking at everybody else. She was uncomfortable, so why didn't she walk out and leave? She couldn't because she wanted to know what I was talking about. You don't get intimidated by people like that when you're real, when you are speaking the truth. You keep it moving. You have sixty people and it's okay that five don't like you and won't come again. I'm never desperate, that's the important thing. I might be invited to give a workshop, and if not I'll try again next year. Nothing is going to stop me. My future is already written, my path is already there. It's right where I need to be.

Susan: And your future is?

Johnnetta: To be an international empowerment speaker for the next twenty to thirty years. The best! That's who I'm going to be. That's my purpose! But I have to be ready emotionally, I have to be prepared. I have to have people in my life who anchor me. People who are going to cry with me, who are going to hang on the sidelines with me. The *real* people. There are going to be fake people all around you too because you're going to get money, and you need to know the difference. It's also important to know your message and stick with it, to always know why you're doing it because things can get mixed and tangled up real fast. I don't know where this journey is going to take me so I need to be ready. I got my combat boots on. I got my gear on. I'm going to need it to get through any weather. There are going to be disappointments, but there's also going to be a rainbow.

CHAPTER FOUR

The Qualities of a Mentor

A Look through the Lens of Our Relationship

In this conversation, Johnnetta and I reflect upon the natural progression of our relationship from student and professor to mentee and mentor, despite the apparent differences in our backgrounds. We discuss what it takes to be a good mentor—someone who helps her mentee explore herself and gives her tools with which she creates her own success. We also highlight key components to a successful mentor-mentee relationship, including boundaries, respect, reciprocity and a readiness to receive.

Susan: How did our relationship evolve to mentor and mentee?

Johnnetta: We were first in a professor-student relationship, but I felt a friendship with you as well by the time your husband died, at the beginning of my second semester. I had been coming to your office to talk about class and started sharing parts of my life with you. When we came back from winter break and you told the class about your husband, I really admired how you handled it. You shared so much, so openly, and you showed a lot of strength. You were so grateful for the card that was signed by everyone in the class. This touched me, and made me want to know you more. Because I admired you, especially the way you always made everyone feel comfortable, even when we were talking about difficult things like abuse or racism. You let us know we could say anything, no matter what. You were always for real with us. And that made my trust in you grow.

Susan: Thank you. I always wanted to create a classroom environment in which my students could openly express their views on even the most racially charged issues, without having to think about censoring themselves in front of a white professor.

I remember asking students in a Human Behavior class to share some of the messages they got from their families. One bright and sensitive young man responded, "I got three messages from my mother when I was growing up: 'Go to church, get a good education, and never bring a white woman home.' When he said that, there were audible gasps in the room, but it was an honest message in the right context. A respectful environment that is steeped in trust can lead to extraordinary dialogue.

Johnnetta: It certainly helped that you had studied the history of African Americans. You also were comfortable with our way of speaking, and you just asked if you didn't understand, without ever taking anything away from our culture. Whether it was cuss words or slang, you accepted us as we were.

You also challenged us. Like the community assignment you gave us— that wasn't easy! We had to go outside to interview clients; it was very hands-on. But it taught us something we could use as professionals later, like when you told us to meet with the client wherever they're at emotionally. And when I walked into Mary Hall Freedom House, where I did my internship, I used everything I learned in your class: how to work one on one with clients, doing things like interviewing them about their situation and making a contract with them agreeing to do or not do certain things as a way to lift expectations. To this day, the practice you gave us makes a big difference in how I live my life. It helps me as a professional, but also as a human being. And, you have the most amazing quotes. Like, "sometimes you just have to take the leap and build your wings on the way down." So many of the things you say stick with me. And students see you live what you preach. You give what you preach. Your being at CAU is priceless. I hope each year someone like me is there, and you help them.

Susan: Looking through the lens of our own relationship, what would you say are the qualities it takes for someone to be a good mentor?

Johnnetta: It takes a special person to be a mentor. It's not just talking on the phone or going to the zoo together. It's opening up places in a person's life that they might not dare to go to and helping them heal from something so deep and so hurtful. It's helping them love them self, find them self, and explore, because there are things about us all we don't know. That's what you do. That's who you are. That's what a real mentor is – someone who gives a person tools. I used to think a person has to be born with it. You don't really know how to do it. It's not something you figure out; it's something you just know. Then I saw how you've taught me and other people to mentor in their own style and give in their own way. I now know that you just need to want to be that person who helps people; but first you need to be humble and learn from others.

We had no rules, really, except to reciprocate. But there were boundaries. That means we respect each other and are honest with each other. We accept each other; this is who you are and this is who I am. Just like that. We learn so much from each other. We cry together, laugh together. There's not a time I have been angry that you didn't hug me. That caring way you have helped me to open up to you. It was really hard for me to say, 'Here's my story,' after numbing myself to it for so long. You allowed me to talk all about my life and my marriage. You let me rant and rave if I needed to. I never felt love from my mother, but I knew it was something important. Love is to me a feeling that comes through the phone when I hear your voice, because it does exist. That's what you are.

And from the start I knew you were committed. Dedicated to me being the best I could be and to our relationship. That's a lot for you to take, my brain and me…and, for me, to take all your writing! You can be a challenge: you can play the devil's advocate, and push me to do my best. I have to work hard with you as my mentor.

Susan: Some people thought we were engaged in therapy. What do you see as the difference between therapy and the committed mentoring relationship that we have?

Johnnetta: Therapy is more one-sided. A therapy relationship goes by a clock. Policies and procedures are more important. They don't exchange phone numbers. The client does most of the talking and the therapist doesn't talk much about herself. With us, you didn't just ask a bunch of questions. We started to talk and you were good at listening, so I decided to open up to you. And you shared things with me: you gave me examples from your own life or professional experiences that helped me learn what I needed to. No matter what I was going through, you would help me look at the good and the bad and would always be fair about it. That helped me make decisions. I left your office with everything so clear.

Susan: I agree with you that I didn't probe in a therapeutic way. I listened, and I opened doors. From there the relationship blossomed into something reciprocal. A therapeutic relationship is not reciprocal. There is a hierarchical structure at the beginning that doesn't evolve like it does with a mentor-mentee relationship. The balance of power is very different, the therapist knows personal things about you, but you know very little about him/her. The boundaries are rigid, whereas in our relationship the boundaries were always in place but changed over time, and our friendship was able to develop. For example, when you were my student I couldn't go out for a drink with you to talk, because there was a boundary that had to be respected. But now I can because you are my colleague. We can meet and talk about the professional projects we are working on, in addition to the many other aspects of life we chat about. Speaking of being colleagues, how do you think being mentored by a professional in your own field has helped you find your own way in terms of a career?

Johnnetta: You are a model I take with me. Like you, I think professional and act professional, because that's who I am. I can handle myself. You helped me value myself, which was my dream. To value myself, and be valued by others. When I battled over the money for speaking engagements, you said to me: "You have your price. If you get five people and four drop off, you still get one. You don't have to take less." When I heard those words I was a changed woman. It was about my worth. You could have said "your fee is too much," but you said, "Girl, you are doing your thing! I believe in you!" So, I left empowered. It stepped my game back up. I got it back together.

Susan: You need to have successes to cushion your falls and to know you can get up again and win. You need something that you've done, so you truly own it. And always remember what you are worth.

Johnnetta: I still feel like a student. I'm still learning from you. Now I'm learning the practitioner side. I'm learning how you've been successful. After our first workshop together, the crowd reacted so strongly. It was beautiful. We did a great job! We knew we had created something special, and we knew we had to do something more with it.

Susan: You had people in tears. They were connecting with you at the emotional level, based on your genuineness, not on superficial characteristics that might appear to set you apart from them. There was a profound connection between you and the women in the audience, though you were from radically different backgrounds. Most were white middle-class professionals, yet the chemistry between you and them was based on something deeper. The identification with pain, need, insecurity, abuse, and not being loved was real for every woman at some level.

The same goes for you and me. Some people think a mentor is going to look like them, come from where they come from and have similar life experiences. But we come from different backgrounds, races, religions, ages, experiences, values – across the board. At first glance, we are two people who wouldn't be expected to connect with each other at any level, and yet, there is this reciprocity that has developed, a powerful bond. What do you see as the similarities that bridge our differences?

Johnnetta: We are both women, we're very feminine and empathetic. We're not afraid to say things, to feel things, to let emotions come, to let emotions go. We are able to look deep into each other and see the beautiful things. If the outer layer stopped us, we'd be in trouble. You and I were able to look past our skin, our ages. Let's face it we don't look none alike. We're able to get past all that's external and see all the beautiful internal qualities that we both have. I'm a crazy fool, but there's a beautiful side of me if you get to know me. I love people and I would do anything for anyone. I'm a go-getter, if I say I'm going to work hard I will. And you're the same way. So, part of what connects us is the passion we both share. We make things happen together! That's the truth. It's just magical. And I feel we are such a great team because you have let me know you too. There is so much to Kossak that people don't know.

Susan: Like what?

Johnnetta: Like you're funny. You are a hard worker; you like challenges and you want change. You're not just a professor. You're more. You care in a whole new way. You're not afraid to know my world. You're interested. I think this is partly because of your professional side as a social worker and professor, but there is something even more important that you have, something special as a human being. Students see it in the classroom; people see it in the documentary. When they see you holding my hand in my DVD about the 12-steps, people could look at me and say, "What is Dr. Kossak doing with that crazy fool from the streets?" You don't have to waste your time on me, let's be honest. You've already been my professor. I've already walked across the stage to receive my diploma. You could throw your hands up and say, "Hey, I don't have time!" But, you want to be here with me, and you make it clear that you get something from me too. When you first said that we give to each other, I couldn't believe it! I thought, "What could I give you?"

Susan: It's a reciprocal thing. I think we're friends, we're colleagues, and we give to each other. It's a very unique relationship. We share our perspectives from where we're coming. For our relationship to have worked, each of us needed to be open to receiving. I think it goes back to wanting to grow: we each were ready to break out of our comfort zones and reach for more, to explore new horizons. Our openness and approachability towards each other, as well as toward other people, conveyed this readiness to receive. From there, you and I, as you say, "got each other." I approached you about writing and presenting something for the Conference of the Georgia Chapter of the National Association of Social Workers, and suggested that we work on something together to help women. You were willing to "check me out" and we clicked. And I learned so much from your perspectives and your story. Our going to Birmingham together to film the documentary *The Road Beyond Abuse* illustrates how our give and take works so well. I expressed an openness to learning about your world and you were willing to become vulnerable and allow me into it. So, openness on both our parts is so important to nurturing our relationship.

Johnnetta: And, I think that being open to each other helps us understand each other on a deeper level, and that helps us truly be real with each other. Like, I know when you get a little pissed, and I can take it. And, I should. That's what friends do. You know me when I get pissed because I get a little loud and I'm going to go off and say whatever and then I'm going to be okay. You allow me to be me. You can't be around someone for three years and not do that. It's like being with a man: three weeks, two months, yeah, he's cute and then he starts getting on your nerves if you can't be you. So, you let me be me and I'm so happy because I feel this year I've gotten to know you more as a person.

Susan: Because the boundaries have changed. The boundaries, although ever-present, evolved as our relationship expanded and you were no longer a student.

Johnnetta: Yes, and that's made it so unique and wonderful! You're the only one in my circle who's a different race, age, religion and it's wonderful. It's refreshing. I rub it in my friend's faces. I do, I brag on you because they don't have a Kossak. You know my husband Willie says, "Your doctor is coming over today!" So, you're my doctor. It's so refreshing to be able to sit around my girls, my age, and talk whatever and I can sit around you and talk shit the same way and it's comfortable. That's unique.

Another thing that's so wonderful about us is in my workshops when they see you my sistahs can say, "Who's the white woman? She was holding your hand. Oh, my God! I wish I had a mentor like that!" I think my friends are a little jealous because they don't have a Kossak. They are all looking for a mentor. It's a whole new level for everyone. One friend will say to me, "I don't have anybody like Kossak who helps me…" And I say, "Yeah, Dr. Kossak helps me, but she doesn't do it *for* me. I did three workshops with her but the other six I did myself." I have to explain this to everybody because some people think it's magic.

Susan: Doing it for you would create a dependency and discount your ability to learn and grow. A mentor acts in a support role: she sees a spark in the mentee, shines a light on it so the person recognizes her own strengths, and provides opportunities to develop those strengths. She guides and supports the process but can't give you the skills. If she did the work for you, neither person would learn and grow, and the relationship would dissolve. This goes back to the importance of *readiness*: each person must be ready to work, learn and grow for the mentoring to be mutually successful.

CHAPTER FIVE

A Two-Way Street

The Essentials of a Strong Mentor-Mentee Relationship

In this conversation we delve further into some of the topics touched upon in the previous chapter. In particular, we discuss the elements that keep a mentor-mentee relationship strong. We focus on the importance of reciprocity— a giving and receiving that works both ways, as both the mentor and mentee have valuable lessons to teach and learn from one another. Johnnetta also explains how important caring, which is revealed through actions rather than mere words, is to nurturing trust between two people. In the same vein, we discuss how important it was for both of us that the other demonstrated a commitment to the work we were doing. Lastly, I share my thoughts on how a mentor does not mold her mentee into the person she thinks she should be, but rather nurtures her talents and allows her, in her own way, to become her own personal best.

Susan: All relationships are based upon some sort of understanding between people. We each have our roles at any given time and these roles are subject to change as the relationship evolves. We also have responsibilities to the relationship if it's going to work well. What are your thoughts about the understanding that underlies the mentee-mentor relationship?

Johnnetta: Acceptance is an important thing. For me it is important to know that you don't judge me in the way family or friends can. Because you are something different, my mentor, I know you respect me and won't look badly at me no matter what I say. That lets me feel comfortable. That's what makes this relationship sacred to me.

Susan: That mutual respect is an essential understanding we have.

Johnnetta: I always respected you. You never said "Hey you're going to respect me or else." But you showed me in the way you stuck to the student-professor relationship until the day I graduated. When I asked you a question about other students who seemed to be having issues in class, or about how a certain professor had voted on some school policy, you would say, "You're a student, so I can't talk about that." That gave me so much respect for you. You kept a boundary by saying that. It showed me you were a trustworthy person; that you took all your relationships seriously, including ours. It helped me to trust you. To know that if I opened up to you, you wouldn't betray me. You would really be there for me.

Susan: I agree, and feel that it is not only a respect for each other that we share, but an overall reciprocity. This is another important understanding in a mentor-mentee relationship—to recognize that the relationship is a two-way street. It flows both ways, and that means giving as well as receiving. In fact, one of the key responsibilities of both the mentee *and* the mentor is to be open to receiving. There is a saying, "When the student is ready the master appears." Well, that works both ways. We learn from each other and help each other grow. This give-and-take has allowed our relationship to evolve and flourish. In spite of our differences, we have become so close, and share a remarkable emotional and spiritual bond.

Johnnetta: I know how important the reciprocity is, especially now that I have my own mentee. We have a great relationship, but it takes so much time and energy to give her all that you have given me. Helping her to get to a place where she actually feels fulfilled when she wakes up in the morning—that is hard work! So, I know how lucky I am to have you! You helped me build wings to fly and pushed that little bird out of its nest.

To do that it takes two people who are willing, honest and genuinely caring about each other. Care and love are not the same. "Do you love me *and* do you care?" Anyone can say they love you. They can buy you a ring. But someone who cares will come over when you're sick and make you some soup, help you pack your things, take you to the doctor.

Susan: So, caring is *love in action*.

Johnnetta: Yes. What I was hungry for was the care. And you showed me that you cared. I remember sitting in your office talking about the abuse. You saw my pain. You would hold my hand. You would allow me to cry, because you cared about what was going on with me. You had empathy. When you are from the streets like I am, you know genuineness. That's what opened me up. Walking out of your office I felt connected, I felt so loved. And not only loved, but valued. I felt better about myself. The thing for me was to feel accepted. My language, the way I wrote-- you got around it. You let me be angry. You let me express shame. You accepted my flaws, all of it. And for me, that's special. If there was ever disappointment between us, we talked it out. That made me so happy, that someone like me was allowed to spend hours with you, telling you my deepest fears. You could have said this is too much pain. You were dealing with your husband's illness! But you cared enough to let me come back. I think we got to bonding because you really listened *with your heart*. Listening with your ears is different. It goes in and out. Listening with your heart is like glue, it sticks.

Susan: So, I was able to tell you a lot, to express my care and concern for you, through my actions. What do you think are the actions that you took that showed me you were committed to your role as mentee?

Johnnetta: I think my honesty about the real me showed I was serious about getting help and being a better person, a better Johnnetta. I wanted someone to guide me to a better place, but I didn't expect you to do it for me. You made me work in and out of class, and I did it. Every week I would have my stuff ready for our meeting. In the beginning, I was nervous about being able to do a good job. When you told me to write a proposal for the social work conference, you gave me some guidelines and told me to start by writing down my story and my 12 steps. I had a lot of anxiety around writing that, but I did it. I came to your office the next week with everything typed up. After a while you didn't need to give me assignments, I just did it. Because I was hungry. I wanted it. So, you had someone who was willing to work on things. Someone who was humble. How can you teach me something if I know everything? Who wants to mentor someone like that? So, I tried hard, but I never expected you to give me so much in return. And all you have helped me to accomplish! I never expected our magic.

Dr. Susan Kossak

Susan: Well, you also have given so much to me. You have allowed me into your world. From you I had exposure to African-American culture that can't be provided by textbooks. I've been able to witness the culture in action. And you give me so much positive energy. The enthusiasm you put into all you do gets me moving. Now you are helping me by participating in these interviews and sharing your thoughts and feelings for my book. So, the tables have turned. It's a reciprocal effect. You are ahead of me now, in that you have advanced in the research process for your own autobiography.

Johnnetta: I'm honored that you think enough of me to share this process and let me share mine with you. I often think how, a few years ago, I was sitting at your desk trying to write a paragraph. I know you always had a deep respect for my ideas, but I never thought this communication degree would kick in. I'm able to market myself now and get myself out there with my workshops. And I'm even writing a book! It's incredible to hear you say, "Hey, what do you think?" Though you've always been like that— you listen to my opinions and suggestions. Every mentor should be like that. For someone else to value your opinion is really something. And it feels really good when you know your mentor can see your hard work paying off!

Susan: It's great for me, too!

Johnnetta: A mentor should want all that help to pay off. She should want the best for her mentee and to see her mentee succeed. But it's still amazing to me when you treat me as a colleague. Coming to my house today with your questions and materials all typed up, it shows you take me and my time seriously. Because in the beginning I saw you as this really big person—someone I never would be as great as, never write or speak as well as. But then the intimidation left, and part of me said: *if I touch her and allow her to know who I am, I could be as great, but, in my own skin.* Every time I left your office, I felt closer to that. I felt freer. And now, I am there.

CHAPTER SIX

When You Love Yourself It's Easy

How to Keep Going, Accept Setbacks and Embrace Success

In this conversation, Johnnetta and I discuss what it takes to be ready to change, and address the question of what it means to be successful. Johnnetta reveals how she stays motivated and keeps moving forward, despite the occasional setbacks and criticisms she encounters. She stresses the importance of continually accepting new challenges and clearly knowing her mission. She shares how vital self-love is to remaining energized, and how releasing the shame surrounding her past helps her fearlessly live her life's purpose today.

Susan: We often talk about the importance of being open to receiving. Only when you are open to receive are you able to change, to accept the help that is given and use it to grow.

Johnnetta: You're right! I say you always have to be ready to receive something, to learn something everyday. I'm ready to receive something from the time I put on the radio in the morning; you never know, something I hear might be the message I need at that moment. And that's what happened with you and me. I was open and I was ready. And I told you that I was ready to receive. I didn't say it was going to be easy or that I didn't need any help. I let you know I needed someone to help me, but not carry me.

Susan: How did you get to that place of being ready for change?

Dr. Susan Kossak

Johnnetta: Waking up in Birmingham day after day with nothing but pain, no-good men, my boys not having an education, I knew that I was in a negative cycle and that something was wrong. Seeing my sister on crack and my mother drunk, I knew I needed to be somewhere else. I needed to change my thinking, my attitude, *and* my environment. I didn't know how, but I *knew* I needed to do it. Failure was not for me. Honey, if I could survive the streets, I could survive a change like this. I knew it had to be better, it couldn't get worse. Moving here to Atlanta, I knew I wouldn't meet the same kind of people as before. I wanted to turn my life around, but I needed guidance. I was starting over at thirty-two, and I met you at that point when I was looking for someone who challenged me to be better and saw my strengths.

Susan: The critical step in getting ready for change was your realization that you were burnt out on negativity. You had hit the bottom, and you recognized that you could stay stuck and buried or you could get out. Where did your strength come from? So many people never make the kind of shift you made.

Johnnetta: It was from putting a value on my life and my two boys, sparing them the grief of the streets.

Susan: I remember you saying you were ready for change, that you knew that whatever was ahead would be better than what you had left. But you didn't just speak these words, you backed them up with actions. You took initiative. You picked up your life and moved to Atlanta, got yourself into Kennesaw State, then into Clark Atlanta, and then you came to my office. All these things you did to create change. You placed yourself in the right environments. You sought the help you needed. And you channeled your energy in a positive way; in class you would do extra for your assignments, and you would help other students. In all aspects of your life, in all of your interactions with others, you demonstrated a focus, creativity, resourcefulness that would take you far. We have been working together for four years now, and you have accomplished so much! How do you sustain your energy and your commitment to keep growing?

Johnnetta: Right now I'm at a great place: I feel so mature, grown, confident. When you love yourself it's easy. I accept myself, and that helps me to do all that I do, because I am not keeping myself burdened by guilt and shame over the past, over things that I couldn't control. That frees my energy! You told me something important when I began to share my story with you: "When the secret is out it loses its power." That's true! Once I started being open about my past, not fearing people knowing the most ugly truths about me, I began to make peace with myself and love myself unconditionally.

And you help keep me moving by always giving me new challenges. You never let me get off easy, but you always, always believe in me. There wasn't a time when you said I couldn't do it. Just the opposite: you were always encouraging me to "go for it!" When you told me I should create a presentation for the National Association of Social Workers (NASW) conference, or work with women because you saw I was so good with my female classmates—things like that show that you really value what I can contribute. That keeps me reaching higher. It feels so good to share all that I have done with you. I couldn't wait to see your reaction to my book. When I was writing it, I could hear your voice encouraging me: "Girl, you can do anything! You already outdid what people gave you credit to do! 12-steps, one workshop, then ten workshops, wow!"

And just the way you came to my house today, with your stuff typed up for this interview. That shows you put in a lot of work, that you take my time and opinions seriously. That gives me energy and makes me feel good. Like when the crowd is with me when I speak, that gives me energy. You know, like you always say, it's a two-way street.

I'm motivated because I have a message. I have a mission. We all have one. You helped me find my message - *that there is something better!* - and showed me the way I could give it to others by using my speaking talents. Now when I give workshops, I feel so good because I am able to tell so many other women that they can change too. And I hope that I really get through to them, that they really listen with their hearts and it sticks. I know that not everyone I will try to help will learn to fly like I did. But even if you reach just one person, it's awesome!

Susan: Johnnetta, you are helping many people. You are serving as an example of how to live a good life, a life in which you balance giving and receiving in relationship to others. I am not the only one who recognizes how much you do for others. Your alma mater Kennesaw State recently presented you with the Phenomenal Woman of Year award for 2009. How did that feel?

Johnnetta: I was shocked. When they called me I thought, "I'm not phenomenal!" I think it's because what I do doesn't seem like work! I just feel like I am living my purpose. I get out of bed and when my foot hits the floor in the morning, I feel it in my gut! It's the most incredible feeling. But when people ask, "how did you get so successful" I sometimes think "*successful?* I don't have a dime!" So when I first got that call about the award, I caught myself thinking: "What have I done really? I haven't even had a job as a social worker!" But classmates are so proud of me. They say "you're doing your thing. You touch peoples' lives." But I guess success means so many things. I had a hard time thinking I was successful, so I started patting myself on the back, saying, "Girl, it's okay to feel good! Girl, it's okay to be da shit! You deserve it!"

Susan: Your dream was to be valued. More money will come. You are paying it forward. Your workshops that make you feel good are helping other women, so it comes full circle.

Johnnetta: You're right. Part of success for me is being able to give back. I do my weekly workshop at the community health center for free, so that I can help others. I have too much to say to be stuck in a cubicle! I didn't want to be a paper pusher for the next forty years. I wanted to help. That's why I devote my life to my 12-steps.

Susan: It's important to recognize that no one else can define success for us. Once your life starts to change for the better, you create opportunities for yourself; doors start to open and choices about what direction to take must be made. You have to remain true to yourself, to what brings you fulfillment, no matter what the outside pressures or expectations might be. What do you say to people when they ask what it means to have "made it"? What is your personal definition of success?

Johnnetta: For me, success means setting goals and working hard to achieve them. It means going the extra mile and never quitting. You pay your dues and reap the fruits of your labor. Success is about never compromising who you are; it's being true to yourself. Success is feeling good about yourself all over. It is liking the person you are at this very moment. Success is the ability to make yourself happy.

Susan: How do you know when you have reached a place of success? Success is a very personal word; it means different things at different times to different people. How can we measure it?

Johnnetta: You are successful when you can see the big picture of what you want for your life clearly, and when you can deliver this vision to other people and they are open to receiving it. Success is when you know in your gut that failure will never be an option. I think you measure success by the lives you touch and change, by your ability to give back to your community. You know you are there when you feel sunshine even when it's cloudy outside.

Success can also be measured by the opportunities available to you. As new doors start to open you have more and more choices to make. Like you mentioned, not everyone might always agree with what you decide to do next, but you always have to stay true to you. I decided that I needed my story to reach more people, and that I needed to write a book. But my life story is about overcoming abuse, and it's not for everyone. Penetration, ejaculation—they're words I use. It says the truth. The book is in your face. I want to be clear and to let other people like me know they can hold their heads up! That they can heal and have a good life despite what happened to them. That is what I say when I speak too, and I haven't had a workshop yet where someone isn't changed because of it. But people have to be ready to hear my message, because it is strong. For me, part of being successful is being me and speaking my truth, no matter what.

Susan: It is true that sometimes people aren't going to react positively to our authentic selves, and sometimes there are going to be obstacles. Setbacks are a natural part of the road to success. But when do you think setbacks become failures?

Johnnetta: Only when we don't learn from them. You need to recognize you've had a setback and learn from it. You have to have a plan B, even a plan C and D. And you have to remember that setbacks are temporary.

Susan: Temporary is tolerable. If you have an alternative plan and are able to view the process from another angle and begin again by using what you have learned, then you've succeeded. You often come back stronger and more self-aware. It is important to go through this process of growth to get ready for success. A crucial part of success is attempting, having that belief in yourself to try. The failure is in not trying at all.

Johnnetta: If you don't experience setbacks, you won't know how to have a comeback, which puts you back in the game a lot stronger. I tell people this in my workshops, and I know this from my own life experience.

Everything I have been through only helps make me the strong woman I am today.

Susan: Johnnetta, you inspire so many people with your honesty and positive energy. People just want to touch you, because you're *real*. Your message is not just about abuse. It's about defining your dreams.

Johnnetta: After my workshops, people say, "Thank you. You made me look at my life in a new way." I've been called a motivational speaker, and somebody who is breaking the cycle of abuse, and on and on. I answer to all of it. People write to me, they ask for my autograph. They say, 'I just can't believe I'm talking to you." I'm so happy to reach my audience like that. I want to always be that approachable.

I'm grateful for what's happening in my life. I know that I won't be done until I'm past 100! Then at 103 years old, put me in nursing care, and let me eat my Jell-O and play bingo! I'll be ready, because I take what you've given me seriously, Dr. Kossak. It's a gift. Being empowered, knowing yourself, having a message—you don't know how powerful that is until you use it!

CHAPTER SEVEN

Defining Your Dream and Developing Your Plan

In this discussion, Johnnetta and I describe an important process through which a mentor guides her mentee: defining your dream and setting practical, incremental goals in order to achieve that dream. In addition to setting realistic goals, we talk about creating a support network of people who can teach and inspire you, and the importance of practicing visualization and tapping into the knowledge of one's emotions when working towards a dream. We also discuss how to break free of the restraints that bar us from attempting the very thing we would most like to do. And lastly, we emphasize consistent self-care, or as Johnnetta puts it, you have to "love the person you're going to become."

Susan: We've talked about how a vital key to success is attempting. The failure is in not trying at all. You need to believe in yourself in order to try, but there is also a practical side to it. You need to define your dream so that you can focus your energy towards it. And you need to have clearly envisioned goals. It's important to think about measuring success in increments, and to set long and short term objectives that can be modified according to the directions in which your life's journey takes you.

Johnnetta: That's why we created the workshop "What's the Plan?" With my first workshop, "Breaking the Cycle," the 12-step model helps people become aware of negative patterns and the changes they need to make. But then people would come up to me and say, "Okay, I am aware, but now what?" "What's the Plan?" helps people take actions to make their dreams realities.

Susan: This workshop starts with defining your dream. On the surface, this may seem an easy thing to do. However, most people haven't really defined their dream for themselves and may be riding on the coattails of someone else's dream. They may not have any idea of who they are and what they want. The difference between a dream and a goal is a plan. What makes the dream more than a mere idea you would like to pursue is your step-by-step strategy for achieving it. Before you can develop that plan and set short and long term goals you need to define your dream. This has a lot to do with why you want to do something or be something. Remember way back when we developed this workshop I said to you, "What was your dream?" You responded, "I wanted to get an education." I replied, "No, that wasn't your dream. You looked quizzically and said, "Yes, I wanted to get an education. That was my dream." I said, "That may be true but that wasn't your dream: it was the means you used to move toward your dream." Why did you want an education? Do you remember what you said?

Johnnetta: I do! I said I was tired of being looked down on. I felt like if I got educated not only would it give me options, but it would let my two boys see that you need options, that you need education so people don't look down on you the way I feel they did to me. And you said to me that my dream wasn't education because you can get educated and still feel devalued but that I wanted to be valued and education was the way to feel valued. It was then, at that moment, I knew what I had to do. I saw how this workshop fit into the bigger picture of what I am here to accomplish. I finally recognized my life purpose: to empower women through speaking, workshops and writing my story. And that changed my life. I walked out your office saying "Okay, that's it!" I realized why I left Birmingham at 32 because until that point I really didn't know.

Susan: Defining your dream is so important to developing your plan because you need to know why. The "why" is going to keep you motivated. What's the reason I am doing this? What is the reason I want this? Why is this important to me? You said getting an education was your dream and I said, "No, it's the means you chose to make your dream a reality." Someone else with the same dream may have taken another path in order to feel valued.

Johnnetta: That conversation in your office was when I saw the light about my own dream. Like you say, it was my "aha!" moment. It really was, because you know I was still searching for my value and my self-worth. When we defined why I wanted to get an education, it became clear to me that I wanted to feel valued. And when you and I sat down and started working on "What's the Plan?" that really put the importance of that conversation into perspective. Do you know how much I love that workshop? I think I love that workshop even more than I love the 12 step workshop. I love presenting that workshop. I can't even tell you the adrenaline rush I get from it.

Susan: It's very action oriented.

Johnnetta: It keeps me in line. I could be sitting here wondering what I'm doing, and I pull out that workshop and it keeps me focused and grounded. It is a great workshop and not because we wrote it. What's so wonderful is that it's for anybody. This workshop is appropriate for a corporation or a welfare agency.

Susan: Well, part of making a plan is creating a support network, and this is appropriate regardless of the field or context. Just like mentorship, all relationships are interdependent, we give to them and we get from them.

Johnnetta: I use the ideas about defining your dream, setting goals, and finding a support network from "What's the Plan?" when I am working with my own clients. I learn so much from my clients and they learn so much from me. They keep me dreaming. The work I do keeps my dream alive.

Susan: You came to Atlanta with the dream to feel valued. You are creating that for yourself right now. You couldn't get it as a child, but you're creating it for yourself now. You are pursuing your education, writing your book and doing empowerment workshops. And you are also recreating your relationships that were destructive in the past, like that with your mother, with integrity and on your own terms. Replacing negative with positive, is certainly making you feel valued.

Johnnetta: That's right! I think it's important to know you can re-create anything.

Susan: It's never too late to have a happy childhood.

Johnnetta: True. And, it's never too late to have a happy adulthood! One of the things I say in my workshops is that we need to eliminate restraints because we set up restraints to hold ourselves back. Time restraints, age restraints… I'll hear things like "I'm going to be fifty and I don't have the time." If you believe statements like that, how can you develop your plan? How can you dream?

Susan: I think we put restraints on ourselves because we've been socialized to do it, and we don't question the reason. Also, we put up blocks as an excuse because we don't truly believe we can accomplish what we want to do. Some people think of every reason why they can't do something opposed to every reason why they can do something.

Johnnetta: And it's easier not to do it. One of my goals this year is to do it! We all get hyped about an idea but when it comes time to sit down and do it, well, that's different. That's why it's so important to define your dream and develop a plan. Then it's real. It's concrete, you put it out there, and you got to do it. It's hard work.

Susan: It's never ending because when you develop your plan steps may lead you in a different direction and you're constantly redefining your action steps. Life is an evolving journey; however, the dream remains constant. The means of manifesting the ultimate dream may take multiple forms but the true dream, your anchor, remains the same.

Johnnetta: Yet what I saw with my clients is that after we defined the dream there was no energy. There was no motivation because there was no vision. That's why I added the step of visualizing your dream before you create a plan. You not only need to say it. You need to *really see it*.

Ten years ago when I came to Atlanta, I packed up my car and my two children and left everything I knew for everything I didn't know. I had to see something in order to do that. I needed to see my future. I needed to see my path. One thing I did envision was me getting out of that environment. I knew where I was going had to be better. I could see that I wouldn't wake up at forty in the same position I was in when I was thirty.

I have my clients create a vision board and keep it in a place where they can see it throughout the day. They have pictures that inspire them to live their dreams. The pictures can't just be of material things. Some can because that's reality, but only a few. They can use metaphors. They have to explain to me what each symbol on their vision board means to them. I have a butterfly on mine because a butterfly starts as a caterpillar and then there's a metamorphosis and it turns into a beautiful butterfly. I have a mountain on my board because sometimes you have to climb mountains. I also have water, which for me represents tranquility. I look at my board and it tells me I better get my ass up and start working! It motivates me.

Susan: The old saying "a picture's worth a thousand words" is true. I have my students do creative visualizations in which first they picture the constrictions weighing them down. Then they imagine a magnet pulling those restrictions off. This helps them get in touch with the difference between being weighed down by the limitations they place on themselves and the freedom of releasing them. Some people don't even realize that they are encumbered until the encumbrance is removed. Then, wow, it's so good to be free to move! We learn intellectually but we also learn experientially through the body, which is the seat of emotion. It's easier to define your dream, to visualize that dream, and to feel that dream in your body when the restrictions are lifted and you experience more freedom.

Johnnetta: The bottom line is you've got to want it. I won't work with anyone who doesn't really want it.

Susan: Define "wanting it" because a lot of people think they want it.

Johnnetta: When I say wanting it I mean you're ready. Your mental state is ready. You're ready to hit humps and bumps. As we say in the hood, you're down.

Susan: How do you get ready?

Johnnetta: You're ready when you see it, feel it, and taste it. You have to feel it in your gut. This is something that's in the very soul of you. Nobody else is gonna' want it for you, so I don't want to hear that you work eight hours and there's only twenty-four hours in the day. You come home and you set aside your time for you. I don't care how, you just do it. I believe that every day you get out there and work your ass off it will pay off! I live it!

Susan: But somewhere along the line their spirit may have been at least partially destroyed. To really want something, your spirit has got to be alive.

Johnnetta: Yes, there's got to be energy. You need to love you. You need to love the person you're going to become. I believe there's nothing I can't do. And I want to surround myself with go-getters because they make things happen. It's important to build a team. You can't be an expert in everything, so create a network of people who you can teach you something, who can support and motivate you.

Susan: How do you feel a mentor readies a mentee to receive these kinds of lessons and encouragement from others? How does someone fully open herself to what the universe has to offer?

Johnnetta: One of the things that you told me when we were coming up with ideas for "What's the Plan?" is "get in touch with your feelings."

Susan: When you tap into your feelings, it's another way of knowing. Feelings bring you information from a subconscious level that you might not have been aware of intellectually. Sometimes we say things that startle us in the moment, because we weren't aware that we were thinking that in our heads; we just felt it. Our first methods of knowing are imprints rather than memories. If a baby cries and someone picks her up and feeds her on a regular basis the baby learns to trust the world as a safe place through experiential learning. That safety is something they feel. It is how we learn trust and is imprinted for life, though as the baby grows up she may not remember why or how she has that feeling of safety. That's an example of the feeling place of knowing. We lose that as we develop the intellect, and often leave that way of knowing behind instead of nurturing the two simultaneously.

Johnnetta: Knowing through feelings is important. I tell my clients that they need to get in touch with what they want from our meetings or else it won't work. They need to really feel that what we are doing is for them. I remind them, "your bio is for you, your curriculum vitae is for you, everything we do is for you, in order to make your dream a reality." They have to really feel that. That's what you did for me. You did it because you care. We did the first workshop together because you cared about my story. And not only did you tell me, but you showed me. You didn't just say "you can do it," you showed me I could do it! You were right by my side during the writing, and you set small goals and showed me how it would all turn into something big. That helped me feel less intimidated.

Susan: Yes, but it is important to remember that I never did it *for* you. A mentor supports and provides opportunities which lead to the mentee creating her own possibilities down the line. A mentor teaches a mentee to open her own doors, which nurtures independence, self-sufficiency and confidence.

But I want to ask you, how do you think people begin? How do they start to believe that they can do it? If we've been sold a bill of goods our entire lives about what we can and cannot do and those tape recordings are so internalized, how do we get to a point in our lives when we say, "Yes, I can!" and go for it?

Johnnetta: That first step is that self-awareness. Again, what we are talking about is getting in touch with your feelings. You could have a mentor, or there are plenty of empowerment programs out there. Really the message could come from anyone at anytime but you have to be ready to hear it. And that comes from going inside yourself and getting in touch with how success would feel to you. If you can taste it, that makes you hungry for it. When you're really hungry, you say "yes, I can" and go for it. You become open to guidance, you take action, your dream happens.

For me at age thirty I didn't know what it was to have a full-time job with benefits or an education because I never had one. But, I did know how it felt to work in a company on a project or just simply win a t-shirt. I did know those good feelings. You have to get in touch with what feels good. And then you absolutely need to know that you deserve to feel good, that you deserve a lot of good in your life.

Susan: Getting in touch with the feeling of good things we have already experienced helps us feel in our bodies how a goal will feel once it is attained. It's a bit like visualization, but with positive sensation and emotion really. We build on past successes and gain energy for future projects that way.

Johnnetta: Yes, but, unfortunately, there are some people we just can't reach—they aren't ready to feel in that way—and really only a few are going to go for it. That's why there are so many more poor people than rich. Somebody sent me a sign that says "Winners simply form habits that losers won't." That's the truth.

Susan: I believe not everyone is ready, wants to be ready or knows they need to get ready. However, there are people who know that something is missing, that there's got to be something more to this life, but they just don't have a clue as to what it is. They are waiting for their passion to drop out of the heavens and grab them. In reality it just doesn't happen that way. They need to start by getting in touch with what interests them and puts a smile on their face. If they love animals and every time they see a little dog they smile, then maybe they should consider doing something with animals. If you're interested in cooking then get more involved in culinary pursuits and then the passion may follow.

Johnnetta: You can watch every chef show on TV. These days, there is something for everyone, for every interest. You can always learn more and get more involved.

Susan: Technology can help you interact with other people and build social networks. There are websites for everything. There is a website called meetup.com. You type in your interest and your zip code and you can find groups focused on any number of different activities and interests. Being around others with pursuits similar to yours, who have their own dreams and goals, can motivate you. Passion is a process not an epiphany.

Johnnetta: And making a dream come true is a process. That's why in the workshop we talk about what success looks and feels like for different people, and then have people actually start developing a plan for themselves.

Susan: The practical piece is developing the plan. Once we know what a dream looks and feels like, we can figure out how to create it. What ways do you need to grow to arrive at that place? If your vision includes laughter, how do you bring that to your life? Say I want to build self-esteem, I have to break the concept down into measurable behavioral actions. What are the components of self-esteem that I can identify? List some concrete activities and actions that demonstrate a positive self-image, and commit to bringing them into your life.

Johnnetta: One of the best parts of the workshop is evaluating your strengths and resources, and teaching people how to use their strengths to develop resources like to learn skills and create a network of helpful contacts, and also to use their strengths to make up for what they don't have. Another great one is the part on self-care, how important it is to keeping you motivated.

Susan: You literally have to take the idea of self-care and figure out what it means to you. Maybe it's, I am going to commit to exercise three times a week, lunch with a friend once a week, getting a physical yearly, or an hour a day of spiritual or intellectual activity that strengthens and reinforces me. There have to be concrete activities that you are going to do as a commitment to yourself. Self-care also includes surrounding yourself always with positive influences and making a conscious effort to stay away from negativity. Self-care should always be in place, and then when benchmarks are reached—like getting a good grade on a test— reward yourself! Do something special: buy yourself a book or flowers or whatever might make you feel good.

CHAPTER EIGHT

Relationships: Girlfriends, Family, Men

In this conversation Johnnetta and I broaden our focus to other relationships. Many of the lessons learned through the mentoring process can be applied to establishing and maintaining healthy interactions with other people in our lives, namely friends, family members, and partners. We discuss how relationships evolve and at times come to a close as each person grows and changes, and how to define and keep our relationships healthy through boundaries, respect, and demonstrated care.

Susan: How do you think the mentor-mentee relationship differs from other relationships, like girlfriends?

Johnnetta: Well, in my own girlfriend relationships there's been the back stabbing. You all are into doing the same things, so you compare yourselves to each other and there is a little envy and competition. I have had four girlfriends for twenty plus years. Like family, it hasn't been all positive. I ran with these women. We had the same mentality. We shoplifted, did men, drank together. When you've been together for so many years a person doesn't want to accept that you've changed and are doing better. I feel I have to work harder to be taken seriously. I feel judged more by these girlfriends, and today I don't feel comfortable telling them everything.

Susan: So, when you have history with someone it's harder because they hold on to the history and particular times in that history.

Johnnetta: Yes! It's easier remembering Johnnetta for who she used to be because they're still stuck there. For me one of the hardest things for the last seven years is to have my friends see me as professional. Maybe one or two can do it. The others want to but can't yet. I had to let go of a friend who I hadn't spoken to for two years. It was so hard. It was so hard to accept that this is what it is and sometimes you have to run the race by yourself and it's okay. After six years, if a friend doesn't show up or say "good job," it's hard to keep inviting them. It took me to 2009 to grow up and accept what every one of my friends can give me. I had to do that for myself. I needed to be honest with myself. This is the best this person can give at this time; it doesn't mean they don't love me.

Susan: In turn didn't you have to say, "This is the best I can give them" as well?

Johnnetta: Absolutely! They are my family of choice. But birds of a feather flock together and when one bird changes its feathers, or changes its course, it changes things. Until I was able to sit down and ask myself what I really wanted, I couldn't understand why they couldn't be happy for me. "Why can't they understand that I'm working my butt off?" Until I realized that this was all each of them could give me, I was upset. I had two choices. I could accept it and love them, or let it break me down and be bitter and miserable.

Susan: So you really dropped unrealistic expectations of them?

Johnnetta: Yes. To be honest with you, it's not fair to hold people to those expectations when you're just going to be disappointed. It's the truth. If you honor and are grateful for the good things that a person can give, you value them. There were a lot of good things. There was a lot of pain but also wonderful times that I can never get again.

Susan: Now you're in a different place to receive different things.

Johnnetta: Today, after our many meetings, I have boundaries. I have boundaries with every single person I come in contact with, even my girlfriends. And I also respect their boundaries more. Boundaries keep me together. In the past, sometimes I could be too below the belt, like with jokes that were too painful. I could be tough, just laying things right out there. Now, especially if a person is really sensitive, I just don't do it.

Susan: So, as you've matured, you've become a lot more sensitive. You don't say, "Well, she's my friend and I can say anything to her."

Johnnetta: Definitely it's a sign of maturity but number one for me was awareness. When I wrote the 12-steps I became aware of my vicious cycles. That was a negative behavioral cycle. Now I will sometimes ask, "Do you want me to lay it out there?" And one big thing I learned was that sometimes you don't say anything. I had a girlfriend who told me, "I want you to just listen. I know what you're going to say, and I don't want to hear it." So, when that friend called me I just lent my ear.

Susan: So, you don't give advice unless asked.

Johnnetta: Yes. But if I hear something over and over I need to say, "Hey, this is draining my energy. I'm in a place right now where I don't have energy to drain. I've given you my advice before and this is what I think. I hope you get it together but this is a conversation I no longer want to have." I need to do that for my own sanity. I can deal with "What are you talking about? You're my friend!"

Susan: So you put it back in their court.

Johnnetta: I can lay it out there and tell you you're a damn fool, but then the other friends will get on four-way and be mad at me. The truth is a hard thing to swallow. They say, "Who the hell do you think you are? You did this and you did that." And I say, "You're absolutely right. I did this and that but look at me *now!* I had to learn a lot. I had to be honest with myself."

Susan: It's not where you're from that counts, it's where you're at. And where you're at and where you're from are two totally different places.

Johnnetta: So for me it's been hard with my friends, but putting boundaries in place with my mother was easier. When I moved to Atlanta I called my mother and told her I was moving and that if she wants a relationship with me she is going to treat me like a daughter. I will say things like, "Momma you're wrong you could have handled that in a better way," or "You need to have a little more patience." And she won't like it, but she respects those boundaries. Then she'll call me back again and she'll say, "You're right, I probably could have handled it better." And she'll call to tell me silly things like she's going to buy a new car. I tell her, "Why do you want to do that?

Pay for the one you've got. Stop being greedy." Then, she'll say, "You're right, thank you." I will tell both my mother and my sister that instead of fighting with each other, we need to empower women today. We need to stand for something. So, boundaries with my mother and sister have been easier than the friendships.

Susan: But, you've worked through forgiveness already?

Johnnetta: I've worked through forgiveness. It wasn't easy. But, it's easier to forgive someone when they are standing up to the plate and saying, "Hey, I've hurt you." My mother hasn't voiced it yet, but her actions say "I've hurt you and I know what I've done."

Susan: She said it in the documentary.

Johnnetta: Yes, she said it in the documentary, but she hasn't said it to me yet. But I know she means it. Hearing it means something, but actions do too. Everyone is not going to give it to you both ways. Like with men, we know they have trouble expressing themselves verbally. That doesn't mean they don't love you. You don't divorce your husband because he doesn't tell you he loves you every day. The actions matter: he works every day, takes you on trips, buys you stuff, feeds you soup.

Susan: That connects to what you said last week about love and caring and that you didn't equate the two, that love is not necessarily caring. Caring is actually love in action. Love can be active or inactive, but what really matters is the caring part, which is love in action.

Johnnetta: Absolutely!

Susan: Well, most people think of love as demonstrated by caring. You know, some people care for you without loving you because of a cause or issue that has connected the two of you.

Johnnetta: I have had the pleasure of having three or four friends for over twenty years. And that is because there has been more love than there has been hurt. And there has been caring, love in action. Believe that.

Susan: That's wonderful, because there are always going to be some bad times, but when the good outweighs the bad it's usually a good relationship.

Johnnetta: The good part is being able to see that there is more good than bad. That takes maturity since sometimes the bad is the only memory left. This is something that you've always said to me: Sometimes people think because a relationship didn't last forever it wasn't real or it wasn't love. It could have been love at the time, but for other reasons we move on.

Susan: Right. If it didn't last forever it still may have been genuine. It was real when you connected, but you grew in different directions. Your needs and interests changed. That person or people were important at that time in your life and you were probably important to them as well. People come into your life for "a reason, a season, or a lifetime." Some people are friends and others are playmates. We need both. Both are positive influences in our lives, so long as we know the difference. We need card, tennis, movie buddies who we play with and don't bond with although we enjoy their company. It would take each of us too much time and energy to nurture every connection as a friend who can be counted on, who we can trust, who's invested in our well being and we in theirs. Yet, it's important to have playmates with whom you enjoy casual activities. It's only troublesome when you confuse your playmates and your friends.

When my younger son was about seven years old we lived in California. Another little boy said some anti-Semitic comments to him. About a week later he was invited to a birthday party. When he asked if he could attend I said, "Sure, but you know Monty will be there. How do you feel about that?" His response was quite insightful: "He's not my friend. I'll never call him or go to his house, but if he's playing with my friends I'll still play. He's not my friend, but he's not going to keep me from playing with my friends." Wow! At seven years old he knew who his friends were. At forty years old he still does.

Susan: You have two sons of your own. How is your relationship with your children?

Johnnetta: My children are my children. I have a different kind of love for them than anybody else. If you're not a mother you can imagine it, but you can't really understand that kind of love. My boys are the reason I get up every day and do what I do. Nobody comes before my children, period. I would absolutely give my life for one of my children, period. I wouldn't even have to think about it. And I would take another life for my children. Believe that. If anyone molested my boys I wouldn't need a judge to sentence them. I would take care of it and get sentenced myself. I probably shouldn't say that, but I'm being honest. I've never come across a molester or a pedophile knowingly, but it's going to happen based on the type of speaking I do, and I'll have to deal with it at that time. As a survivor, those are some of the things I think about, though I don't dwell on it. But I guess this is where a lot of my own pain comes in, because my mother didn't protect her children. I've asked her, "All these people you cut up and put a brick through their heads, why didn't you put a brick through my uncles' heads? Because they were blood? Because they were your brothers?"

Susan: What did she say?

Johnnetta: Nothing. She just says she didn't know. "Well, when you found out why didn't you go and put a brick through one of their heads? Because at the time, if you were going to put a brick through someone's head, that's who you should have done it to!" And I asked her, "Why didn't you protect your little girls?"

Susan: She didn't respond?

Johnnetta: She just says, "Well, things happened to me." I don't accept that. A mother will do anything for her children. You are there to protect your kids, period. Yesterday I was watching the nature channel. There was a lioness with two newborn cubs. This lioness Momma was hungry and had to go get something to eat. So, she hid the cubs in the bushes. But, of course, they wandered out. They wandered out toward the crocodile pond, and she heard them crying. She had a choice to jump in the river and save her babies and risk being killed or stay safe. She jumped in the water with crocs all around her. She didn't even look side to side. She just swam across the water. She got across that river and was able to save her babies. As a woman and a mother, I was just blown away. The crocs had every advantage because she was alone, but she was ready to die for her babies. That is an animal, but what do we do as humans?

Susan: Not as much, sometimes. Many people are not in healthy relationships with their kids.

Johnnetta: I told someone this story the other day because they are having a hard time doing the right thing. They have a husband, bad things are happening, and the kids are hurting. So, I asked her, "What are you going to do?" Are you going to tread that water for them babies?"

Susan: Usually the lioness hunts, lies on the prey, and waits for the male lion to come down and eat, then she and the cubs eat what's left. But as you saw on that show, there are rare occasions when the male lion will step out of his role to help the female, as when he brought her food because he saw she was struggling to hunt. That is a great example of how nature adapts to circumstances and eventually evolves, and a metaphor for how family dynamics are shifting in society. For humans, not long ago it was just the mother in charge of the children and the fathers were pretty removed. That's fortunately changing and many times the father is the primary caretaker and nurturer of the children and certainly would die for his children.

Johnnetta: If a father's not providing for his kids, then I would take him in their room when they are sleeping, have him take a good look at them, and say "Honey, they deserve love, warmth, and your care. It's no longer just you and me." If that approach doesn't work then, baby, you better swim across that river and fight if the daddy lion won't fight for you!

Susan: Tell me a bit about your approach to your relationships with men.

Johnnetta: A lot of people think the way I think about relationships with men and love is harsh. I do what works for me. You have to do what works for you as long as you're treating the person right. If you don't know how to treat a person right, you ask them, "How do you want to be treated?" I ask many women I see, "Did you tell the man how you wanted to be treated?" And they say, "Do you?" I say, "Yes, nothing is wrong with telling the person how you want to be treated. It's ok to say, 'Hey, I don't like the way you spoke to me. I feel bad when you say these things.'"

Susan: You're making a big assumption that people are aware enough about how they want to be treated, not just how they don't want to be treated and that they're assertive enough to share that information. And a lot of people aren't.

Johnnetta: True, a lot of people aren't. I meet a lot of women and they don't know they can say this and that. I say, "What do you mean you didn't know?" One of the things I have to say is, "Why are you afraid?" You can start by saying the things you like. When my husband and I go shopping I say things like, "I really like pajamas."

So, I'm telling him all the time what I like. So, when he goes and buys me two pairs of pajamas, he's picked up on that. He knows this is something that she really likes. For me, little things matter. I do! Most people know that about me. So, if you like money, if you're a gold digger, then you say "I like money." If the guy doesn't have any money then say, "Nice to meet you" and, you keep walking. You meet someone and they tell you they don't like children do you think they're going to want some? Or do you think they're going to want them around? So, you're going to be left with babies. Am I right? One of the things I find about women is that they say, "Well, I thought he would change." No, no, no! One of the things about me, Johnnetta, is I don't have a problem telling you how I want to be treated, and I don't mind you telling me how you want to be treated. If you come to my house every week and you want me to have your favorite drink for you, then I'm going to have your favorite drink. Just like you and I have a great relationship and if you say to me, "I'm going to meet you in my office next week and I need you to have your 12-steps done." Well, I'm going to have them done.

Susan: Besides your current relationship, which one has been the most memorable in terms of what you have learned?

Johnnetta: A guy I dated was a pimp and messed around for years, yet it was the best relationship I had. My best friend said, "How was that the best relationship? He hit you. He messed around. How could that be the best relationship?" I was so happy to be able to say, "You know that's one thing to look at. But, I was in the same place as he was then, so I didn't see it. I didn't care." That doesn't mean there wasn't something special about him. I never said it was a Cinderella story. I said it was one of the best relationships because I had learned something. I learned the value of me. And I got a checking and savings account. He always talked to me about saving money. And whatever I did, he supported me. I remember being in massage school, and he brought me lunch. When I graduated he was there—the only person with gold chains around his neck, but he was there. He was the only man in my life who showed up every other night at 7:00 p.m. with food, took the boys to get their haircuts, and took them everywhere. So, that's what I mean about him being special. I try to focus on the good things because the bad things were so small by comparison.

Susan: Was he your pimp?

Johnnetta: No, not with me. I don't need a man for that. He was one of the most beautiful people I ever met in my whole life. He was a giver. He took the kids on the streets to get their hair cut before school. He fed the homeless. He had his ways, but he was a beautiful person. He was the definition of caring. If I was sick, he would bring me soup and feed it to me. He would say "I'm going to the club, but I'll be back in an hour to see if your temperature is okay." That was one of the best relationships I had. When I walked away from that relationship I was able to have a checking and savings account, pay my bills, and pay them on time. He wasn't a monster to me. He did things that I didn't like, but I accepted that. Never, ever was I forced to do anything I didn't want to. For me, today, I honor that.

Susan: So, what made you decide to leave him?

Johnnetta: Well, we only got into two altercations in four years. He is a person that valued me. He respected my boundaries. He knew that he wasn't going to come over after 9:00 p.m. because I had two boys and I wasn't going to be fighting. We respected each other. We didn't show disrespect in public. I wasn't going to be like my mother. I pretty much knew some of the things that I wasn't going to tolerate. He pretty much stepped up to the plate. I want to say I weighed all that against the two altercations we did have. The first was when he thought I was cheating, and he thought someone was over the house. And the other one was because although I never saw him with another woman, I heard about it. When I consider everything, I still say he was the one who helped me mature and become the person I am today.

Susan: Part of your resiliency and how you survive is that you take the positive from relationships no matter how large or how small and choose to hold that more closely than the negative. Not that you forget the negative, but you choose to hold the positive more closely.

Johnnetta: Well, you build up hate if you don't. You begin to see everyone as hateful.

Susan: It's like changing a mindset so that when you go into a relationship you don't say, "I'm never going to get in a relationship with a man who smokes, drinks, or does this or that." Instead you enter a relationship knowing yourself and what you want. You focus on the positive things, the things you *do* want rather than the things you don't want. Then you get into a relationship with a man who is loving and caring.

Johnnetta: Absolutely, and after this relationship I knew in the next one what I wanted. I wasn't going to tolerate a man who hit me. Hit me today and we divorce. I know that about myself now. I'm happy I learned so much from my past relationships because a part of my story and how I empower women is to say "Okay, you got pushed down, pushed around. You got two or three baby daddies. It's okay. It's not the end of the world. It doesn't mean you have to stay down."

Susan: When you say that to women do they take it as if you are minimizing or discounting their feelings?

Johnnetta: Actually, that hasn't happened to me. When women come to me they are pretty low. They've heard my story from articles and the DVD. They know I've been through it. They know I got out. They know I have left abusive relationships, and they want to know how. They know I have experienced the negative side of relationships. The women who come to me for advice are appreciative women, desperate women. They want to know: "How did I move?" or "How did I get out of the relationship?" But the biggest question is "How after seven years are you still focused? How did you not stray from your path?"

Susan: And your response is?

Johnnetta: My response is that my dream, with your help, was clearly defined. I wanted to be valued. Leaving that relationship meant a part of me wanted to be valued. Moving here was a part of being valued. I didn't know at that time where I was going, but I knew something had to be better. Even in relationships. Friends said, "You're not going to leave him. What about all the trips and stuff?" I told them, "Honey, you go by and see him. He's yours now." I wanted something different than the way I had lived for thirty-two years.

Susan: Speaking of your first thirty-two years, in recent years you have made so many great changes. Yet, as you mentioned, you have worked to maintain friendships with women who have known you for twenty years, even though at times it has been difficult, even harder than your relationship with your family. To you, what's the difference between family relationships and close friendships?

Johnnetta: You choose your friends. You get stuck with family. The difference is that one is blood and one is not. Honestly, that's the difference. For me, my friends were absolutely my sisters.

Susan: One is blood and one is not. What is the importance of the blood connection?

Johnnetta: I love my friends more than my family. I know that may be a "no, no," but it's true. Although, I read somewhere that most people like their friends better than family. For me, family has never been number one. Because I didn't feel like I had a family. There was no close family connection. I didn't have a lot of family to love. My family didn't love me, so my friends' families were the closest to family that I've been around.

Susan: So, it was easier to forgive your mother even though she didn't protect you or take care of you than your friends who are not related to you and didn't hurt you to the degree that your mother did? Why do you suppose this is so?

Johnnetta: For me, the word *easier* doesn't fit in that sentence. It wasn't easy. I would say I felt more comfortable forgiving my mother. But, I know what you are saying.

Susan: Do you think it's because you weren't invested in your family and didn't care about losing them and you were more invested in your relationship with your friends?

Johnnetta: I can say even with everything that happened between my mother and I, I never stopped loving her. She was my Momma and all you know is your Momma. I loved her the only way I knew how to love her. I don't think it was a mother-daughter love. And I'm still learning how to love my mother and that may take the rest of my life. But if my mother and I lost contact it probably would be easier for me than if I lost contact with my friends. My friends take a stronger toll on me than my mother. They are my family. That's the way it is for me. I can't say that I love them more than I love my mother, but it's different.

Susan: Why can't you really say that? Because society says that you can't?

Johnnetta: No. Even though some horrific things happened, she is still my mom and I know it's weird, but I believe she did what she could do. I'm not saying she did the best she could. Because she'll say, "Well, I did the best I could." And I say, "No, you didn't. You only did what you could do at that time. But, you didn't do the best you could have." I won't give her that. There were times when she drug us through the storm with her, but at least she didn't totally abandon us. I do love her for that. I do give her that we had some place to stay and we never missed a meal. I do thank her for that. But my friends and family are different. It's a different kind of love. My friends and I are there for each other. We can be catty sometimes, but we also protect each other. They never abandoned me.

Susan: Love and conflict are very different, but both keep us bound to people through the strong emotions they provoke.

Johnnetta: I remember you explaining something to me that put everything into perspective and helped me have a better relationship with my girlfriends. You said that anger and hurt are the same emotion. One manifests outward and the other manifests inward. They are just different ways of expressing the same feeling. Angry people are hurting and hurting people are angry. And sometimes people need to feel something to keep a connection to a person, and with some people anger bonds them because they are unable to express hurt. My sister, Sonia, keeps that going with my mother. Sonia goes out and smokes crack all night and blames Momma for it. She tells her it's because of her that she smokes the crack. It's her way of not taking responsibility, but it's also a way she stays attached to Momma.

Susan: Yes. Part of the problem is projection and some is based in history. However, there's another part of her that wanted a close relationship with her mother, which is natural, and since she didn't have it she maintains a connection to her in a negative way. The pain of no connection is greater than maintaining a negative or angry connection. If it weren't, she'd break ties with her.

Johnnetta: True. As for me, I would rather hold on to a positive connection with my mother than a negative one. Not for my mother but for me, Johnnetta. I could easily have a really negative connection with her, but I choose not to. I'm okay with the way things stand because my mother has nothing she can give.

Susan: What has kept you connected to your mother after you dropped the anger and you've forgiven her? Why not walk away from the relationship?

Johnnetta: Well, I didn't get angry with my mother until I was in my thirties. My sister was always angry with her, even as a little girl. I blocked out the way my mother treated me and all the horrible things that happened to me until my thirties. Anger was not an issue because I didn't even think about it. Coming up the way I did, you just loved your mom. That's just the way you were taught. Then in my thirties I started thinking about what happened to me and thought "Where was my mother?" Then there was anger, but not enough to stay with me day and night. So, the way I'm able to have a positive relationship with my mother at this point happened when I moved here and started taking control of my life. I just said, "No more. I'm not a child anymore." I told her how I was going to be treated. I set boundaries. It's been eight years and only once or twice has she overstepped her boundaries. I really mean that. So, it works for me. I know she loves me the best she can, and I realize I can only love my mother the best that I can. I can't go back to being five years old and getting that kind of love a child needs. I'm forty. We respect each other in a mother-daughter kinda' way, and for me, it works.

Susan: You said your sister has always felt the anger. She needed a stronger connection to your mother from the time she was a small child and the only way she was able to do that given the circumstances was to maintain the anger.

Johnnetta: It's hard not to feel the anger. It sounds like I'm making it up when I say I am not angry. A professional might say, "Oh, you've got to be angry sometimes. It's got to come out some way. You were powerless." Well, I'm not powerless now. I know what I feel and anger is not me. I feel sorry for my sister. A lot of things happened to her. She has a right to be angry. I tell her it's okay to be angry today. And one of the boundaries I set with my mother was not to ever tell me to shut up when I want to talk about anything. She owes that to me. I don't bring it up all the time, but when I do she listens to me. She still drops her head. There's a lot of shame there, but she's not defensive anymore. For me, that boundary means I can speak about it when I need to, and that keeps me from keeping it bottled up and then getting mad.

Dr. Susan Kossak

Susan: It sounds as if you are categorizing your mother's strengths from her weaknesses. We all have both strengths and weaknesses. You are choosing to love the strengths and not to focus on her limitations. I believe being able to do that puts you in control of your emotions and the relationship.

Johnnetta: I couldn't have put it better. There's not a lot of good about my mother, I'm sorry to say, but there is some. I think my job is to educate her about herself, point out her strengths to her. She's a great cook. So, when I go home we cook something. She loves to go fishing, so we do that. This summer she drove from Alabama to pick me up and bring me back to her house. She wanted to do it. She worked hard the two weeks I was there to be positive, to be nice. It was a part of my mother that I never saw before. That visit is a happy memory, and I need more happy memories to replace the ugly ones.

Susan: So, what I always say, "It's never too late to have a happy childhood," is true!

Johnnetta: It's never too late.

CHAPTER NINE

Dealing With Conflict

In this conversation, Johnnetta and I approach the subject of disagreements, which are natural occurrences in all relationships. As Johnnetta candidly describes a misunderstanding that we had, we see how conflict, when handled in a healthy manner, can help us learn about each other and make the relationship even stronger. We highlight how boundaries and misperceptions generally lie at the heart of conflict, and how valuing both oneself and the relationship is the foundation for resolution. We also discuss letting go of unhealthy relationships and highlight the importance in all scenarios of focusing on solutions and sharing concerns in a direct, yet sensitive, way.

Susan: We've talked a lot about relationships and the many components associated with healthy relationships. However, we haven't talked yet about a natural occurrence in relationships, namely conflict or disagreements and how we bridge those disagreements and keep the relationship at the same emotional or professional level. I'd like to ask you, since we are using our relationship as a lens for most of these conversations, to talk about some disagreements or conflicts that you and I have had and how we've either come to a resolution or we've simply agreed to disagree. Talk about the process. What were these disagreements about and how did we resolve them?

Johnnetta: Well, first of all, when you're working closely sometimes you're going to rub each other the wrong way. But I don't see too much wrong in you! (Laughter.)

Dr. Susan Kossak

Susan: It's so hard to be perfect!

Johnnetta: It *is* hard to be perfect. Let me clear the record. I have known you four years, and you haven't changed. You're a great person. But getting to know you was like first love, you know, how at first everything is good. Then when you get married you wake up and say, "Hey, what happened? I didn't know you had a bump right there!" So that's how it was for me in our relationship because I saw myself as a student. I saw myself as the person that was learning. I didn't realize that our relationship was reciprocal until you told me. I always felt it was one way. Not that you made me feel that way, it's just that for me in my life at that time it's what I needed to know. In other relationships, I was always the leader, even when I was acting crazy. The way my mother was, I had to lead all the time. Then my big sister got on drugs, and I had to be *her* big sister. So, when I met you I was at a point in my life where I didn't want to be the big sister anymore. I didn't want to be the leader. I wanted to humble myself and sit under somebody and learn. I was starting over. It was a new me. In order to be a new me I had to learn some things. So, when you came along I wanted to treat our relationship like in a way that would help me learn, I wanted to chill out and let you help me. I needed that at that time. I was willing and I was ready, and it takes a big person to stand back and let go of having all the control.

Remember, when we met I didn't know anything but the street. You knew more about academics, and I thought you knew more about life. So, at first if you said something I didn't agree with, I would never tell you. I always thought that you knew what you were talking about. I felt there was no way I could be right. If things bothered me, I just shook it off as the best thing for me.

I can recall when we were working on the DVD of the 12-steps, which was the first time I remember being upset about something you said. It just kinda' ate away at me. I don't remember exactly what it was but it was something to do with my 12 steps, and I felt like "I worked my butt off for this! How could she say I didn't do something right?"

Susan: I remember the comment. I mentioned that you didn't go through all the 12 steps during the taping. How did you come to feel your performance wasn't good enough from my comment, which I felt was a neutral comment, not a criticism or a compliment?

Johnnetta: That's where conflict comes in. That's how *you* felt. The comment was neutral to you. But, now that we are sharing about our conflict I can only be honest with you and tell you that it didn't come off that way. Did I think you were putting me down? Hell no! But, something didn't click right. That's the first time I remember feeling a little awkward with you. I value you so much that to me it meant I didn't do good enough. It made me feel once again in my life I wasn't good enough. Know what I mean? I felt like "I don't ever want to do a workshop in front of her again because I'm going to always feel that I'm missing something." I had all these emotions going on. But, then when I watched the DVD I thought it was wonderful. And I just let it go. I always knew you wanted the best for me. I never felt you wanted to hurt me.

Susan: So, when conflicts occur are you saying the best thing to do is to let them go and not deal with them?

Johnnetta: The best thing to do is to stop and take a deep breath and get to a place where it is quiet and you can think about it and look at the part that you played and say, "Ya know what? I'm going to call her and we're going to talk." Because if we don't, the conflict will be like a parasite that gets in there and gets comfortable and buries itself until it comes back up.

Susan: Because something triggers it. So, we're both in agreement that when something is bothering you and you value the relationship, you're going to address it with the other person.

Johnnetta: Yes, though it's easier saying than doing! It's hard to say something especially when you really love someone and you really respect them, but you're also really trying to set your boundaries. It's easier said than done. I know because I'm living it. But I'm at this time in my life when I need to be honest. That means being able to open my mouth and say, "This may be silly and doesn't mean anything to you, but it bothers me."

Susan: Is it harder to be honest with yourself or with another person?

Johnnetta: It's harder to be honest with the other person for me. Let me tell you why. I know me. I know what's irritating me. I know what the problem is on my end. But telling someone about it can be harder, especially if the person is defensive. It's not only defensive people, but meek, humble people that you know are doing all they can do for you. It's hard to tell them, too, when you know they wouldn't do anything to hurt you. Also, it can be difficult with a person just like you, with a strong personality. Two people with strong personalities are really the hardest, but I like a person with a strong personality because I get it! I have always been the type of girl who appreciated the truth. I didn't say I always like it. That's a different story, but I've always been able to appreciate it. Growing up knowing that my momma didn't want me, I had to numb that part of my life to keep living, so I'm the type of person who numbs out to things. I am numb to the negative feelings, the emotions, but I still hear the message. I block out the negativity. I don't let it stop me.

Susan: We've said it's important to address conflicts with people you care about in order to maintain and perhaps strengthen the relationship, but it's a very difficult thing to do. You talked about that one incident in our own relationship. Can you share a bit more about how you handled it?

Johnnetta: I didn't handle it because I didn't bring it up until we had a different little conflict. I didn't bring it up because what happens is I think about something and say to myself, "Is it worth it?" It may not be worth it to me, but it can be worth it for the next person. That's the truth. While I never brought it up to you, I never forgot it either. I think one of the other times that you and I were having a conflict was when we started doing workshops together. I remember I was talking to you after we spoke together at Mary Hall Freedom House, where I did my internship. Something about my background had come up and you said something I wish you hadn't. You didn't say anything wrong, you were just telling the story. Well, I wish you would've asked me. So I told you, "I don't want you saying that." You said, "Well, like you say, "Let's keep it real." That was the very first time you spoke to me on that level and it made me very angry. I was so heated and let me tell you why. It's because I never wanted to go on that level with you because that's the ghetto, alley, low-down dirty level, and I don't like to do that street stuff. It took me back to my street days. We do keep it real, but on a nicer level. But, your voice, you said, "Let's keep it real!" I said, "Okay sistah, no, no you don't want to keep it real with me because we can keep it *real*." I didn't want to sink to another level with you, and I was so afraid because I never want to lose our relationship. You have seen me get upset, but you have never seen me show my ass. Hope that you don't, but believe me, you push the wrong button and you will see that. So, when you said that I was so mad because then I felt like you was one of my friends from the street. And, we're harsh. I said, no I can't talk to Dr. Kossak like that. We ended up getting it together. And, what you said was, "Well, it's your story and you need to get ready for it." You said that. I said, "You're absolutely right but here are some parts that I'm not ready for." And, we ended up getting it all together. You said to me, "I'm glad you told me because next time I'll check with you beforehand even if I think it's already out there." That was the first conversation you and I had about boundaries. I'll never forget because for me that was a good thing. After that conversation I have boundaries with everybody. And I learned that we can't assume that we know what we want each other to say about us. That was a great thing you did for me.

Susan: Boundaries are vital to healthy relationships. How have you resolved conflicts that occur in other relationships such as with girlfriends, your spouse, or in business? How are they similar and how are they different?

Johnnetta: When you're having conflict with your girlfriends, they're your girlfriends so it's more personal. It's usually about something stupid with me and my girlfriends. Like how someone's shoes looked or how someone looked fat in their jeans. It usually stems from somebody's envy, so they say something that's below the belt. And, then we talk about it and we let it go.

My conflicts with my girlfriends have gotten so much better now. I only speak about things that need to be said at that time. I give compliments, and if I can't, I shut my mouth. I've gotten past the place where I need friends to help me build my empire. God will give me the people to build my circle and the only way it's gonna' happen is that I'm gonna' do it! So, I don't feel that betrayed feeling towards my girlfriends like, "Where were you? You said you were gonna' be here!" If you show up that's wonderful, but if you don't my name is still on the marquis, baby! I am going to make it even if I have to go it alone.

For business, you got to put your business hat on. You have to have tough skin, period! You have to know when to talk and when not to talk. You have to know if you're gonna' work with this person on a business deal or walk away from it. That's the bottom line. That's how I see it. I'm not gonna' force anything I have on people or allow anyone to force their product on me. I'm not gonna' compromise in a way that leaves me feeling bad because at the end of the day I have to wake up with me and my ethics and morals so, everything I do is for a reason. If it don't make money, it don't make sense. If it's silly, I don't want to be a part of it. I'd rather work on one great deal that's gonna' give me five thousand dollars than work on nine that are bullshit. I'd rather walk away with my name intact, feeling good. I can do something for free and still walk away feeling good but, I'm not doing anything right now that doesn't benefit me and what I stand for. That's just the bottom line for me. I'm prepared to pack my briefcase and walk out of meetings. I'm prepared to say, "This won't be for me today." So, in business it's about finding something that, as you always say, is a win-win. It's about relationships, but you don't have to like everyone. They may be good at marketing you. You may be good for their product. You take what you can get out of it, and you be the best professional you can be. If you reach a point where you can't be that, you move on. I'm not desperate and beating down anybody's doors. I believe my message will stick. So, for me when it comes to business, I don't want to burn bridges. I want to be neutral, "Hey, how are you? It's nice hearing from you." That's it for me.

As far as family and home and husband, I'm just gonna' say it. We talk and there are also some things I don't say, but I try to be one of those people who don't hold onto baggage. That's crazy. I like to let go of things. For me, in order to do what I do in my life in a great way, I just can't afford to clutter my brain up.

Susan: It sounds as if you avoid conflict by not letting negativity rent too much space on your brain.

Johnnetta: That's right! Once I realize where I stand with someone and where our boundaries are, then I don't want to go there anymore. What I mean by that is that when I figure out that you and I don't work good at this, then we're not going to do it anymore. If I figure out that you and I work good at this other thing, then I'm gonna' say, "I think you and I can do this really great." But if I see there's conflict, I'm not gonna do it anymore. It just keeps me happier. I love my friends, colleagues, business partners, and I love people in my circle. It takes work to keep a twenty-year friendship. But I don't expect friends to cut their life short for my vision. And, I'm willing to go every step of the way by myself if that's necessary. I don't feel, "You weren't there and you coulda' came!" Who am I to tell you what you shoulda', coulda' done. I believe real friendship will be there at the end. You don't have to look for it. It will just be there. They will just be there, if they can, because we all have a life. I want to be that friend, too. I want it to be reciprocal. I don't want it to be all about me. I want to be there when your book comes out. I want to be there to see you at your workshops. I want to travel with you if you're going on a business deal. I don't have to say a word. I just have to be there to show you that same support that you show me. That's a real friend.

I think that as I keep growing all my relationships and boundaries will be safe. I need to know my place sometimes; I've shared that with you. I'm forceful, I'm loud, I'm over the top. I cut people off. I'm really good at taking over. I would take over someone else's spotlight. I've done it! I've been told that before and it's not cute. So, I'm learning to shut my mouth up when it's not my time. I will pinch myself and sing and think of other things to stop myself.

Susan: You've learned to keep it moving because you don't have time for unimportant disputes. If someone can help you, that's great. If not, she or he better get out of your way.

Johnnetta: Right on, Sistah! I shared my feelings on conflict because I know how it is to be fighting all the time. I was a big ball of conflict all by myself. I'm serious. I was the shit starter! I was the friend who told your secret to the other four. When you came in I was the first person to laugh at your shoes because they didn't look like mine. I laughed at you because you didn't have the curves I had.

Susan: So, that was because of insecurity.

Johnnetta: It was insecurity. It was thinking more of myself than I should have. It was wanting to be the biggest all the time. It's true. I was always the party person. When I walked into the room, it was a done deal. I was that type of person and it was ugly. Me and my friends all did it to each other for twenty years and it was ugly. I was the leader. No one else will say it, but I'll say it. I really was ashamed of it, but I'm practicing not being that person. If I can't say something good, then I don't say anything at all. If I need to say something to you because it's vital to our friendship, then I'm gonna come to you and say, "I really need to speak to you, and I'm gonna accept what you tell me." And I might not hear the answer I want. If you say, "I don't care how you feel that's just the way I am," well, I'm gonna' accept that but I want you to accept that I'm not gonna' be in your life. I have to say, "We're still friends, but I have to back away. You have a good life." I don't want anyone around me that I need to cuss and fuss and argue with. I don't want anyone in my life who I got to hit, hurt, criticize, put down. I want somebody who when I see your name on the phone, I light up.

Susan: So, part of dealing with conflict is not dealing with negativity unless you absolutely have to.

Johnnetta: Not everything is negative. Some things have to be said. Some things can be negative but are true. And some things come across as negative, but they aren't meant to be. But we are human, and conflict is gonna be around until we die. And I'm sure you and I will have other conflicts during the rest of our relationship.

Susan: I hope so.

Johnnetta: Because that means we're normal. But I hope we'll be able to talk about it, laugh about it, and keep on hugging each other. That's the great part because I'm never gonna grow and get better if I don't have the people around me that help me grow and get better. I need people who tell me, "You were wrong, Johnnetta." I hope you'll always tell me when I'm wrong. Even if I throw a damn tantrum, tell me because that means you love me and you care enough about me to not let me make an ass out of myself. I value you. I trust you. You are, I have to say, one of my major players.

Susan: I'm a player now! (Laughter)

Johnnetta: You're one of the main people in my life that I really trust. I know you wouldn't screw me, and I know you wouldn't let nobody screw me. If something's going on, I can lay down my head at night and say, "She got me! I'm gonna wake up in the morning and it's gonna be okay!" And, that's big.

And I appreciate so much that you and I were able to talk about our conflicts. Afterwards, I had a lot of emotions, but I felt so much better. It just goes to show that you and I are friends and that we love each other. There are a lot of things about us that are different, but we learn from each other. And there are a lot of things alike. Our worlds are far apart and yet it's amazing how we are passionate about so many of the same things.

Susan: What do you see as our similarities and the passions that bond us?

Johnnetta: The similarities, well, we're fighting the same cause in our own ways. Those causes are loving a person for who they are, giving someone a second chance. People deserve second chances because that's what I got. And, the belief that there is someone special out there for you. When I say passion I mean because you and I working together has brought both of us to a whole new level. Our careers have expanded and we've taken this in a whole new direction. Don't you agree?

Susan: Yes, I absolutely do.

Johnnetta: I remember that workshop when I was talking about you and how I met you, and that lady in the audience said, "Dr. Kossak tell us how you feel about her and what she's taught you." And you said, "Wow, where do I begin!" So, our passions overlap. We're still doin' the same thing: I'm talking about empowerment and loving yourself, and, you're talking about the same thing when you're talking about the power of us. *Power* is a big word. *Us* is more than one person. It's you and I. And you give other people the courage to find that power. We both have a platform. You have a teaching platform. I'm speaking on the stage. Honey, we're giving the same message. The beauty of it is that we're showing the world that here's two people, one from the mean streets and one from the middle class, pulling together to make love. Because that's what we made, a love baby! (Laughter)

Our baby is that message. That message that it doesn't matter how you look, it doesn't matter where you come from. The message that the future is right here, that you feel your purpose for being here in your bones. And the amazing part of the message is to enjoy the journey.

Susan: You're going to enjoy your journey. Wow, we talk about the process being the product and now you're living it.

Johnnetta: I enjoy it! I like working hard! Things that would bother the average person, are usually so silly to me. Where I come from everyday is a struggle. I don't know who's gonna' come in my room and touch me. My momma might flip out any day now. Be ready. Sleep with your clothes on. I'm serious. I think that I was built to travel down this road and I cannot be successful unless I work for it. See, my story is like a movie that's gonna' be made in five years. I can't make the movie if I don't live it!

CHAPTER TEN

It's Never Too Late

Nurturing A Relationship With Self

In this final conversation, Johnnetta and I discuss the vital relationship which lies at the heart of all other relationships: our relationship with self. Here, Johnnetta takes the lead and interviews me about what I have learned firsthand about having a healthy relationship with myself. One of the key points to come across is how a healthy relationship with yourself prepares you to both receive from and give to others. Indeed, it is the primary foundation for building healthy relationships with all other people who enter your life. Having a healthy relationship with yourself requires consistent self-care, and Johnnetta and I discuss how we put this into practice in our own lives.

Johnnetta: Dr. Kossak, what do you have to say about having a relationship with yourself?

Susan: For most women of my generation the thought of having a relationship with yourself was a disassociative idea. It was not in most people's consciousness. Your life was essentially planned. It amounted to a series of developmental stages based more on societal norms than on self-awareness. You grew up, got married, and had children. These were not decisions you made. They were "givens" for most of us. They were the expectations of what an adult did. At a certain age range those were the tasks you needed to accomplish to move to the next period of life and be fulfilled. It was a chauvinistic time. You catered to your husband

and children and if they were happy you were supposed to be happy. If your children did well, then you were successful. There was very little consideration of self. It was all about how you reacted to other people and how you supported other people. The sense of self kind of got lost, assuming, of course, that it was ever present.

When my children grew and left the nest, I found myself asking, "Who am I?" and "What do I like?" This was a change from asking, "What do my children like and what does my husband like?" I did a lot of introspection. Counseling for me was one way of doing that. I learned a lot about myself, particularly when I got out of my head and into my gut. The type of counseling that helps you get in touch with what you feel rather than what you think was the most helpful for me. Another thing I did was explore what my interests were, and then I got involved in those emerging or buried interests. It was also important to continue my education. I came from a family that wasn't very educated. Education was never emphasized. My father, although he had a successful retail business, never graduated high school, and my mother never went to high school. I was the first person in my immediate family to graduate college.

I went to college for three years, quit, got married, had kids and then went back and completed my final year of college. Afterwards, I taught grade school and high school. Then I decided to go back to school for my Masters degree and become a social worker. By then, I had gone to counseling and gotten to know who I was and what I liked, and that process was very enlightening. After I earned my MSW I worked in various social work positions for many years and then returned to the university to earn my Ph.D. in social work and began teaching at Radford University in Virginia, which is where I taught before coming to Clark Atlanta.

Johnnetta: You said something very interesting. You said you became a social worker because you went to counseling and learned about yourself. What made you go to counseling? Because from where I come people think, "Why do you need someone to tell you what you think?" Counseling is not thought about or encouraged in the African-American community. I've always been so impressed with white Americans because you guys will go to counseling. And if I had that or my mother had, gosh what a difference it would've made!

Susan: Well, we all have our skeletons in varying degrees with our families and their conflicts. I was aware from my education and life experiences that your family is not objective, and a lot of the messages you get from your family, including the self-fulfilling prophecies, are not accurate. We internalize what other people say about who we are and we play out those roles and they're not always satisfying. We don't even know where we got the idea of who we are and what we should be. When I was a kid, if you were a woman you were a secretary, teacher or nurse. And, you were only supposed to work until you married or if your husband couldn't afford to support you on his salary alone. There was no consideration of what might be fulfilling to you. I realized that particularly when I went back for my Masters degree and got information about different forms of counseling, particularly Gestalt. I later went to a Gestalt workshop, where you learn the model by working your own "stuff." It was a five day retreat in North Carolina. I was extremely uncomfortable there. I remember going to this session with a Gestalt instructor where fourteen other people were sitting on the floor with no back supports. I went into the room and immediately pulled up a chair behind everybody and sat there. I thought, well I know this separates me from everyone else, but my back bothers me when I don't have back support. I was sure that was why I sat there. As the training continued I was getting more and more uncomfortable as I watched people work through their personal stuff with the psychiatrist who was running the group. Everyone was just sitting around, not saying a word, just listening. I said to a colleague, "I'm leaving. This is very uncomfortable." He said, "No, stay. You need to work your stuff."

Well, finally the next day I said to myself, "I either need to work my stuff or I'm leaving." I decided to work. I got up there and sat on the floor next to the psychiatrist. I closed my eyes just so I would block out everyone in the room. He asked me things about my childhood and for some reason in the course of sharing incidents from my past I mentioned that I always wanted a box of sixty-four crayons. He asked me why I wanted that particular box of crayons. If anyone had asked me when I was a little girl or even up until the time of this session I would have said because it had the silver and gold crayons. It was the only box that did and little kids love the glitz. However, what came up for me as I was talking to him and picturing this box of crayons in my mind's eye was the flesh color. I pictured the crayon box with this one crayon, the peachy flesh color, rising to the top. I then turned to him with my eyes closed and said, "Because it had the flesh color." I immediately opened my eyes because I was so surprised by my response, because it came from my gut not my head. Wow! It was really an epiphany for me. Just moments before I had been sitting in the chair behind everyone, and what I really wanted was the flesh color, symbolizing the connection to other people. And then we went through an awareness exercise: I always knew that my brother was the favored child, and just tried harder and harder to please my parents. The instructor asked me what it would have taken for me to be fully accepted and special in my family and I responded, once again from my gut, "I would have to be born a male." Once again, wow! That was an impossible thing! I had to let go of it and it was a relief to do so. Before I sat down, the instructor asked me to make eye contact with each person sitting on the floor watching. There were fourteen people sitting around. Those were the same people with whom I thought I could never share my personal life, but I could now feel their positive energy. I remember thinking that I could never have done this without them. I made eye contact with every single person in that room and many of them were crying. Then I went to sit down and without thinking about it, I sat down on the floor.

When the session was over we had a break and one woman came up to me and said she was happy to see me sit on the floor with everyone else. I thanked her but proceeded to tell her that the only reason I was sitting in a chair before was because of my back. She looked at me in a very kind way and said, "We all choose our level of discomfort." That was very powerful for me because my back still bothered me. It wasn't as if I saw the light and my back no longer bothered me, but it bothered me more to be separated from the group by sitting in the chair than it did sitting on the floor without a back rest. So it was a realization: I had been creating a wall, consciously or unconsciously, which was preventing me from getting a need met, from connecting to these people." So, that workshop provided an epiphany, and I knew that I needed to go to counseling to learn more about myself and how I might be sabotaging my self-actualization. That was the start of my-*self* exploration.

Johnnetta: You know, you have really, really taught me something. The other day I was talking about you and our age difference. I look at you and I think "I have so much to live for!" I see your energy and that you're still a diva. I call you my diva. You always look good. You've got a swagger. On the street, that means you got it together. You got your money together, your career, your mind. It's a good thing. So, I always say "When I get to

Dr. Kossak's age, my swagger's gonna be like hers!" And that's something to look forward to instead of looking at my mom who just turned sixty and is almost deader than a damn door knob. Life has beat her down. But, to look at you and I doing all the things we're doing! You still haven't slowed down. You're still learning stuff about yourself. And, when you said to me, "I never thought that I would be writing a book and walking through the doors that are opening," I thought that's a wonderful thing. Everyone should always be walking through new doors.

Susan: It takes a long time to figure your journey out. I would periodically go to counseling when I was at a crossroads or to learn something about myself. Then I went through a trying time when my husband was diagnosed with cancer and was sick for five years before he died. I had to work to support us and care for him. It was difficult to see someone deteriorate in that way despite the fact that the last twenty years of our marriage were pretty rocky. We grew apart and were probably not suited for one another from the start, but circumstances put us together. For various reasons, we hung in there for forty years. That's quite a long time. I didn't know me when he died. I was so busy taking care of everyone. So I went to counseling once again and was fortunate to have a very good counselor, a social worker. She helped me get in touch with myself. I did some self-care by taking the summer off from teaching.

Johnnetta: How long ago was this?

Susan: It was four years ago.

Johnnetta: So, as you say, "It's never ever too late."

Susan: I say it's never too late to have a happy childhood.

Johnnetta: You taught me that!

Susan: There comes a time when you have to mourn what didn't happen and the lost expectations. God knows my life had some tragedies, but my childhood was not nearly as traumatic as yours. Yet, everything is relative.

Johnnetta: Yes, it is.

Susan: Sometimes there comes a time when you have to parent yourself.

Johnnetta: Yes, you do!

Susan: You just have to say "Now is my time! I'm going to parent myself and do whatever it is that I want to do so long as I don't harm anyone else in the process. Now is my time to make myself happy."

Johnnetta: Do you think happiness is a choice?

Susan: Yes, absolutely! Absolutely happiness is a choice, and it's a very personal choice. Happiness for you may not be happiness for me. We have control over one thing in our lives: How we respond to what has happened to us. We can't totally control what happens to us. We can influence it on some level, but we can't totally control it. We can, however, control our response to it.

Johnnetta: I can agree with that.

Susan: And we can control what we choose to own and what we choose not to own, and what we allow to rent space on our brains.

Johnnetta: I've learned that from you, too.

Susan: And I've learned that when you make an assumption about something—because an assumption is our guess and not always our best guess— make two other assumptions and pick the one that makes you the happiest. I try to do that.

Johnnetta: Yeah, you do!

Susan: I worked with people who had eating disorders, particularly compulsive overeaters. Most people wanted to take a pill and miraculously be fifty pounds thinner the next morning. They didn't want to go to workshops, counseling, or exercise classes. In other words, they didn't view weight loss as a holistic process. They usually said, "I'll be happy when I lose the weight." They're not interested in starting anything new in their lives until they reach their goal. What happens is that even if they do lose weight, they're not happy if they didn't go through the process of gradually changing their self-perceptions. They look in the mirror and they may look terrific but they say, "Who is this?" It's hard to change your perception of yourself overnight, especially if, for better or worse, your identity was tied to being heavy. They look in the mirror and they've lost an entire person. And they usually gain the weight back and wonder why. If you bleach your hair platinum blonde after being dark-haired all your life you may look great, but you're not going to feel that it's you. But, if you gradually dye your hair a shade lighter each month, soon you're platinum blonde and don't remember when you went from dark-haired to light. You've had a chance to become comfortable with the change.

Johnnetta: It's important to be able to be yourself. I'm comfortable with wearing wigs. I put my wig on and think I look like a hot mess, but I get lots of compliments on it. But I say, "Hey everybody I got this new wig on so bear with me because the microphone they gave me goes over my head and messed up my wig." I'm hot and sweaty and there's too much going on. Then I relax and everybody relaxes, because I put it out there. I'm so happy that I can be me and am okay with it.

Susan: When we're comfortable with who we are we give everyone around us "permission" to be who they are.

Johnnetta: We always want acceptance from other people, but you gotta' accept yourself first.

Susan: But before we can accept ourselves, we have to first know ourselves.

Johnnetta: It's self-awareness.

Susan: A lot of who we think we are is what other people told us we were. It's not always who we really are.

Johnnetta: Absolutely!

Susan: Self-awareness involves peeling the layers of who we are and what we think and how we feel from what we've been told to be, think, and feel. I keep discovering things everyday that need re-examination. The goal is to keep peeling those layers away until you get at the core of who you are.

Johnnetta: You have to get to a place in your life where you have a "just fuck it" attitude. Do your thing and other people get on board or they don't. And you're okay because you know you're not hurting anybody. You're just loving you inside and out. When do you get to that place?

Susan: I think that's one of the luxuries of age. You get to a point where you don't have the need to impress other people. You may not be climbing the career ladder anymore, so you don't need to act in a certain way. You don't have young children whom you're concerned about embarrassing. If you're married or in a relationship you've reached a point where you're not as focused on how your behavior affects everyone else. Because even if you are not directly hurting another person, there can be concern about the perceived morality or the perceived ethics of your behavior. You wonder whether your actions will be perceived in a negative way by others. Note that I said the perception of others, not what you value as good or appropriate. We've been socialized, particularly women, to be overly concerned about the perceptions of others and to weigh them over our own values and ideas about what is right. You get to a point where you say, "Enough! I want to consider how my behavior affects me based on who I am. I don't want to hurt anyone, but the primary person I need to please is me!"

Johnnetta: Not secondary, primary.

Susan: That's right! And, it may on the surface seem selfish, but it doesn't matter if it is or not. Do you like to be around a martyr, someone who always sacrifices herself for other people? They're often mean, bitter people. They're uptight people. Who wants to be around them? What kind of joy and love do they spread? When people are relaxed, laughing, and having a good time, who are they hurting?

Johnnetta: You know, Dr. Kossak, that's exactly how I live. I don't want anybody in my circle, especially personal, who drags me down.

Susan: It's not an intellectual decision. You feel it! As you get older and have more experience with yourself you learn to trust your gut. And if it doesn't feel right, don't do it!

Johnnetta: You're right! And it's true with taking on a client or a workshop. If I feel "Uh-oh I'm not feeling good about this," then I don't do it. I'd rather have my integrity than five thousand dollars.

Susan: Why be miserable? Life is too short to be miserable. You can potentially make up the money you spend or give away, but you can never make up the amount of time you devote to someone or something. We each have X amount of time on this earth and we can never make up the time we give away, so you want to make sure you used your time in a positive way. You can't give your time to other people, which is an admirable thing to do, unless you give your time to yourself. You can keep writing those checks to charity, but you'd better put some more money back in the bank or the well will run dry. And unless you give yourself something back emotionally and physically after giving of yourself there won't be anything else to give. Yet, we equate self-care with selfish. I wonder if lack of self care is productive let alone wise.

Johnnetta: My mother is an example: she couldn't give to me because no one nurtured her, and she didn't know how to nurture herself.

Susan: Right! Don't wait for anyone else to anticipate and fulfill your needs. Don't put off giving to yourself, do it today! Be your own best friend! Buy yourself flowers!

Johnnetta: There's so many ways to care for and motivate yourself. Find that favorite song or put on those jeans that make you look bootyliscious or that new dress that makes your curves stick out or buy yourself a Victoria Secret bra. I've got a friend who wears nothing but Victoria's Secret bras. Honey, I got a Victoria Secret bra, a Wal-mart bra and a thirty-dollar Sears bra that's all right, but I tell you, there's nothing like that Victoria's Secret bra! Honey, you're worth it!

Susan: Well, Maya Angelou says, "Every woman needs a black lace bra."

Johnnetta: Absolutely! That's why I'm doing the "red stiletto night," a workshop that teaches women how to be intimate with themselves. Not just in a physical way but in an emotional way, too. Self-motivation comes in many ways. I got my favorite song and my favorite person I can call on the phone. Some people don't have that. You got to set up those things that are gonna give you strength. I feel like I could pick up the phone and call you at four o'clock in the morning and say, "Dr. Kossak, I got a great idea. Girl, cut the light on!" You know how many people don't have that? That is major to have. You need that friend who is always gonna perk you up. And you need the friend who is gonna kick you in the ass when you need it. You need someone who will say, "I think you could've handled that better" or "I think you were a little selfish." That's better than agreeing with me all the time. I need that. People need that. Don't you agree?

Susan: Yes, I do. Sometimes the physical or material things you just mentioned serve to trigger feelings of self-awareness, which leads to self-motivation. Motivation comes from within but it can often be catalyzed by an external experience. The more we open ourselves to the world the more we learn about ourselves.

Johnnetta: You're right.

Dr. Susan Kossak

Susan: What we both essentially are saying is that you need to create an environment that is conducive to knowing or creating yourself. You can't do it alone. You need to be around positive people and get rid of the naysayers who think of every reason why you can't, rather than every reason why you can. Be around people who are accomplishing things in their lives. They don't have to be the same things you're accomplishing, but these people will have an energy about them that is contagious. Energy is contagious. A positive attitude is contagious. Stay away from the negativity. I think your suggestions are great. Find the poem that motivates you or inspires you. Find that song that you enjoy. If you're feeling down, put on a bright color rather than putting on something dull. Take a walk on a bright, beautiful day. Do something that is uplifting. Be around uplifting people.

And remember, before you can create yourself you need to know yourself. Not find yourself, you're there. From that point you grow. The person you are today is not the person you were five years ago and is not the person you will become five years from now.

Johnnetta: I created myself.

Susan: You surely did. You knew some of your strengths and you knew there was something better out there. You knew what you needed to keep going, like your poems and your music. That allowed your spirit to remain strong and to get some of the resources you needed.

Johnnetta: I knew my strengths and I also knew my weaknesses. That's important too. I moved here seven years ago, and that's when I really started living, and when I really started learning to self-care.

Susan: That physical change from one place to another symbolized a rite of passage for you. It was like a line in the sand. You crossed over. Now you had to stay on your chosen path. In reality, the change had started long ago in Birmingham. It was something internal that began to prepare you to make the major move to Atlanta.

Johnnetta: When I hopped in that truck and pulled away from Birmingham, that was my "aha!" moment. That's when I started becoming the Johnnetta I am today, because I knew I couldn't be the same Johnnetta I was leaving. My whole mentality had to be broken down and rebuilt. I'm still breaking it now. I'm still a little ghetto and I'm the first person who'll say, "I'm in recovery." I'm looking for the next seven years to be even better. What I love about our relationship is the continued growth, all the positive changes. We're both just getting better. And the wonderful thing about doing this book is that we've learned so much more about each other. These conversations are bringing us closer. Every time I hear you talk, I'm learning more about you as a person, as a professor, a friend, a mother, a speaker. It's amazing to me how willing you are to put yourself out there.

Susan: You need to say to yourself, "What is the worst thing that can happen by putting myself out there?" We could argue that there is a boundary issue and that everyone should have healthy boundaries. When a boundary issue presents itself you need to ask "What are the rewards and risks of putting myself out there? Is it ethical? Will it do more good than harm?" Then, make your decision. Some things don't need to be shared. It's not that they are necessarily deep dark secrets; it's just that it serves no purpose to share them. There are always things that we might want to keep to ourselves. I believe it's healthy to have something that is just yours. And it's not because you're ashamed but rather because it's yours and only yours. It's personal to you. Your thoughts are your thoughts and don't need to be shared with anyone unless they serve a purpose and you want to share them.

Johnnetta: Absolutely! There are some things that we are just dying to get out. We can't wait to say something at a workshop or with our friends just to see if another woman feels the same or has done the same thing.

Susan: And when you aren't sure about whether you want to talk about something, or when you don't know what you're feeling, I usually tell clients to describe how their body feels because your body never lies to you. You just need to learn to be aware and read it accurately. Put whatever feeling you're experiencing in the context in which it's happening and you'll be able to know what's happening inside of you. For example, you may be experiencing butterflies in your stomach and your heart is palpitating and that could be a pleasant feeling of excitement or it could be nervousness. You're not sure what emotion it is. So, you say to yourself, "What's going on around me?" I put the bodily feeling in the context in which it is happening and better understand what I'm feeling.

Johnnetta: I am so glad you taught me that. I used it just this morning with some anger I was feeling.

Susan: So we can say that to get to know yourself you need to get in touch with your feelings. And you do that by getting to know how your body feels. If you're not there yet, you can do breathing exercises, engage in meditation, use creative imagery, or take a yoga class to get in touch with your body and in turn with your emotions. Hang with positive people. If you don't know many positive people, join a group dedicated to one of your interests and keep trying different groups until you find the one or two that feel right for you and offer healthy support. Recognize that you can't go through this world alone and that you need to arrange for positive support systems. Also, make sure the space where you live and work is positive. Set up your environment to be friendly and welcoming to you. Include your favorite songs, flowers, and items that trigger positive feelings. You may want to develop some rituals for yourself. You might light a candle and walk from room to room symbolically cleansing the room and starting anew. You may choose to rearrange some of your furniture to create a more open, welcoming atmosphere in your home or office. Do whatever you can to allow the flow of positive energy. Make a change. Let some fresh air into the room and into your life.

Johnnetta: And, never think it's too late to make a change! Never let age stop you.

Susan: Right! So what if you're ninety-two and you go back to school. You're learning and not sitting around waiting to die. You're alive as long as you choose to be alive. We need to do whatever we can while we can regardless of age. If you can't do one particular thing, then do another. If you don't have any interests, perhaps you have a friend who does. Join that person and if you don't like her interest you may meet someone else who can introduce you to a new adventure. Get to know yourself. Know what interests you, where your strengths lie, where your challenges lie and where your heart is.

Johnnetta: It will save you a lot of pain and misery in the end, and bring you a lot of happiness throughout the journey.

Susan: Right! Then, as you always say, "You won't wind up a woulda, coulda, shoulda, bitch!"

Johnnetta: Absolutely!

Conclusion

Here We Are, So Now What?

As I finish compiling the conversations that make up this book, I find myself more than ever in a moment of enjoying life's many gifts. As a tenured professor at Clark University's Whitney M. Young Jr. School of Social Work, I continue to teach and mentor students, which serves to sustain my belief in the human spirit. I also am collaborating with a production company in designing a program about creating and sustaining healthy relationships, with a focus on mentoring. In the spirit of this book's title, *Reaching In, Reaching Out,* I am facilitating programs for women focused on a healthy relationship with self, which in turn allows one to give to others. These programs guide women through the process of looking within themselves to acknowledge their strengths and then present them to the world quite naturally. It also helps them understand how the universe provides for us through those very people whose lives we touch when we use these talents.

Johnnetta continues to touch and change lives through her empowerment workshops and speaking engagements. She is also busy promoting her new autobiography, *Rising Above the Scars,* and exploring options for a feature film about her life. In addition to these individual projects, Johnnetta and I continue to collaborate in an effort to help women define their dreams and create their plans of action through workshops and consultation services. We are expanding upon this original workshop series and taping it for electronic distribution. We also are designing a workshop for teenagers and young women to help them establish their own "floors," or bottom lines in terms of behaviors and attitudes, so that they don't fall into an abyss of destructive cycles.

Dr. Susan Kossak

Like most women, I have experienced many different roles and relationships: daughter, sister, wife, mother, mother-in-law, grandmother, lover, student, teacher, social worker, professor, consultant, speaker, and now author. Each role and time in my life had its positive and negative aspects. I am convinced that had I known myself earlier, more positives would have manifested in my life. During the time in my life when I didn't know me, I wasn't aware that the people and things around me were gifts. I wasn't interdependent, but rather thought I had to be a self-sufficient "superwoman." I lost precious time pursuing that idea. Now, I so greatly appreciate the value of being helped by and helping others, of working collaboratively with people of diverse talents and in turn sharing my strengths, I decided to write a book about it. I hope that through the process of reading *Reaching In, Reaching Out,* you have come to a better understanding of what it means to mentor. Mentoring is action and communication; it is a relationship which is shaped by two distinct personalities, and which evolves over time. In my own relationship with Johnnetta, I found that the mentor becomes the mentee and back again; it is this reciprocity which sustains the relationship.

Writing a book about mentoring has been a soul-searching, enriching, and at times frustrating process. As I've reflected on Johnetta's and my relationship, I have looked back to where we were four years ago and seen how our relationship has evolved and strengthened. This has reinforced my own belief that the universe provides the people we need when we are ready to receive. As the preceding chapters explain, our task is to ready ourselves for what the universe will bring us by nurturing our relationship with self and taking action on a well-defined plan. Through the process of compiling my conversations with Johnnetta for this book, an important theme has become clear: never lose sight of why you are striving. The *why* is more important than *what* your goal is, because this is what keeps you motivated when you hit inevitable bumps in the road. The *why* reminds you of the importance of your mission, of what it means to you at the heart-level. I believe this *why* is so important, that it currently is the focus of the workshops and talks I deliver.

I included other relationships in addition to mentoring in this book to illustrate the commonalities among all human relationships, as well as to illustrate the fact that a fruitful mentorship entails the "readiness" of both parties. Success in our own lives means interconnectedness with others, willingness to learn, and demonstrated sensitivity, caring and respect in our interactions. When we have achieved this, we are masters of both giving and receiving support and are ready to mentor.

My own mentoring "seeds" were planted long ago: it took life's ups and downs and much personal growth for them to blossom into my present life of building bridges, reaching out, living my purpose. This became only clearer to me recently. As I was culling through old greeting cards and other "paper memories" I came across a poem I wrote when I was eleven or twelve years old. My own faded penmanship transported me to my bedroom in my family's New Jersey apartment, and I saw that even as a child I understood the value of mentoring. As you read the words I wrote as a young girl, you, too, will know that my relationship with Johnnetta was "meant to be."

I need guidance in all ways
To help me through my troubled days,
A light to shine and show the path
Of truth and right and not of wrath.
I need guidance to make me feel
No guilty conscience as my meal.
I want to think I'm doing right
In all my days with all my might.

Dr. Susan Kossak

Some Frequently Asked Questions on Mentoring

Below are answers to some of the questions I hear most frequently from others about the mentor-mentee relationship.

Q: Where do I find a personal mentor?

A: Wherever you find yourself, figuratively and literally. Seek people to connect with through your interests, school, clubs, in the grocery store, parties. Like attracts like, but not based on superficialities. We attract people who are on the same level of emotional development. So, get yourself ready to receive from others. "When the student is ready, the master appears." How many times has a friend told you something you were not ready to hear? Then, someone else tells you the same thing and you have an "aha!" moment? You heard it when you were ready to receive it. Get yourself ready emotionally through ongoing self-care. Separate from negative people. Acknowledge positives in your life and your own strengths everyday. Focus on solutions not problems. Socialize with positive people, pursue an interest, design your own ritual for healing, develop a spiritual side, move outside of your comfort zone and grow. Your mentor will often appear when you are ready.

Corporate or business mentoring is somewhat different. Often times you are assigned a mentor. If you desire a mentor and are not assigned one, familiarize yourself with people in positions to which you aspire. Based on my research, women choose mentors based on the mentor's present position, where she *is*. It doesn't matter as much to women where she *came from* or if she is similar to her. Men tend to prefer mentors who came from similar backgrounds and *made it*. If the male mentee came from the *streets* they don't want an affluent, ivy-league graduate to mentor them.

Network and make connections. Then, when you find someone to whom you relate, ask that person to be your mentor. If the person's schedule allows, he or she will likely say "yes." You empower people when you ask them to be your guide, teacher, or mentor. And thus begins a win-win relationship.

Q: How do I become a mentor? How do I know I am "up for it?"

A: Personal mentoring in certain ways is different than corporate mentoring. As a personal mentor you are a life guide. Sometimes you begin the relationship in that role, perhaps through paired mentoring programs and/or through social service organizations such as Big Brothers, Big Sisters. If you are committed to helping and learning and you accept the mentee as whole and valuable the relationship is likely to evolve and strengthen. In a less "arranged" or formal scenario, the mentoring relationship starts as an association between two people, which develops into a bond of mutual respect through the initial support of the senior member and grows into a trusting circular relationship. You know you are ready when it *feels right* and both parties are benefitting.

Q: What qualities should I look for in a mentor or mentee?

A: When I was interviewed by Georgia Public Broadcasting Radio, the commentator asked, "What was it about Johnnetta that attracted you?" My response, which came straight from my gut, was: "She was someone I could learn from." The commentator looked surprised and replied, "You could learn something from her? But, you're the mentor, not the mentee. Isn't she supposed to learn from you?" Her question and my response reinforced my belief that mentoring is reciprocal; that you need to respect the mentee and be willing to learn as well as teach. This dialogue also reminded me that the important things to look for in either a mentee or mentor are:

- Can I learn from this person?
- Is this someone who I hear and who hears me?
- Is this someone I can trust?
- Does our connection feel right?

If you answered these questions positively, then go for it!

Q: I am a new mentor. How do I go about setting boundaries?

A: Boundaries should be discussed in the beginning and conveyed not as walls but as respect for self and the other's space. The best way to establish boundaries is through being open about them from the get-go and role-modeling them in your own life and throughout the mentoring relationship.

Q: How organized does the relationship have to be in terms of meetings or assignments?

A: Organization or structure is individualized depending upon the relationship and setting. It will be more structured in a new relationship and/or a formal setting. Johnnetta and I started our relationship as student and professor; while she was a student we maintained a different type of structure and boundaries than we have now that our relationship has evolved and she is no longer my student. Structure is a method of setting boundaries and can be adjusted as the relationship transforms.

Q: I feel my mentor is pushing me too hard lately, and she doesn't understand all the pressure I have at home right now, how do I tell her?

A: We are constantly learning our pressure points as we learn more about ourselves. Decide what you *can* do that is challenging but not nerve wracking. Tell your mentor what you *can* do now and what you will do as your attention is not diverted by other issues. Emphasize what *is* possible rather than what is not possible now.

Q: What if I fail? How do you meet expectations of the other and of the self?

A: Johnnetta likes to say, "Failure is NOT an option." Set challenging but realistic expectations. Step out of your comfort zone but don't set yourself up for failure. Consistently reevaluate your goals. If they are too easy you won't reach your full potential. Also, remember that we can't reach everyone. Not everyone is ready to receive or able to give when you connect with them. Be honest with yourself. For the mentee, be sure you are working to your utmost and allow your mentor to encourage you to reach your goal. If you are invested it will work. For the mentor, never be more invested in your mentee's achievements than she is; otherwise, you are only pushing your agenda and not hers.

Q: How and when do I end a mentoring relationship?

A: Relationships end when one person grows for a sustained time and the other remains stagnate, or when two individuals grow in different directions or try to stifle each other's growth rather than support it. Sometimes, we have come as far as we can and need to let go so that when we take stock of the relationship we can count it as positive. People sometimes lament "it wasn't real because it didn't last." But healthy relationships are not always meant to continue indefinitely; that doesn't mean they weren't valuable. Two people connected at a time and place in their life journeys and then took other paths but still were instrumental in helping each other reach that juncture.

That said, when you no longer are hearing one another and contributing to growth it may be time to pass the baton. Signs that this is happening present themselves in the form of missed meetings, ongoing excuses about not completing work, constant negativity, one person demonstrating a dependency rather than an interdependency for a sustained period, or when the mentee reaches a plateau and both people are "spinning their wheels." To end the mentoring relationship in a healthy manner, meet to discuss the successes you've shared, how you've overcome adversity and where you both are now compared to when you started. Tell each other what you've received from the other. Discuss what the mentee needs from this point forward. The mentor can offer suggestions to the mentee about moving forward and receiving guidance from another source, and perhaps arrange a meeting with someone who could travel the next path with the mentee.

www.ingramcontent.com/pod-product-compliance
Lightning Source LLC
Chambersburg PA
CBHW020011050426
42450CB00005B/418